# INVESTMENT DECISIONS
# IN SMALL BUSINESS

*Small Business Management Research Reports*
*Prepared by the University of Kentucky for the*
*Small Business Administration, Washington 25, D.C.*

PUBLISHED UNDER THE UNIVERSITY
OF KENTUCKY STUDIES PROGRAM

# INVESTMENT DECISIONS
# IN SMALL BUSINESS

## MARTIN B. SOLOMON JR.

*Instructor, College of Commerce, and Research*
*Assistant, Bureau of Business Research*

*Prepared by the* UNIVERSITY OF KENTUCKY
*under the Small Business Administration*
*Management Research Grant Program*

*Project Director:* JAMES W. MARTIN
*Director, Bureau of Business Research*

UNIVERSITY OF KENTUCKY PRESS
*Lexington, 1963*

# FOREWORD

*This study* has been conducted and prepared under the direction of James W. Martin, project director for the University of Kentucky. The research was financed by a grant made by the Small Business Administration, United States Government, under the authority of Public Law 699 (85th Congress).

Only a limited number of copies of this report have been printed. It is available for reference in any of the Small Business Administration offices throughout the United States or at many reference libraries. Copies of the report also may be purchased directly from the University of Kentucky Press, Lexington, Kentucky.

Summaries of this study are being printed and will be available in reasonable quantities. These summaries may be secured from SBA field offices or from the Small Business Administration, Washington 25, D. C.

The Small Business Administration assumes no responsibility for the accuracy of the data contained herein, nor does it necessarily endorse any opinions, conclusions, or recommendations which may be a part of this report.

John E. Horne
Administrator
Small Business Administration

# ACKNOWLEDGMENTS

*I owe* a great debt to the many people who have contributed to this volume:

To the businessmen who participated in the interviews, for their time and interest;

To the many people who read early drafts, for their comments;

To the research team of Bernard Davis, James L. Gibson, Lawrence Goodman, Robert Haun, and Dale Osborne, for their help and thoughts in the collection of case material;

To James W. Martin, for his splendid editorial assistance;

To Judy Shewmaker, for her alert and painstaking secretarial work;

To my wife Mary Ellen, for her patience and understanding;

But most of all, to a man whose unending search for truth and whose wisdom, tenacity, imagination, and insight become a forceful inspiration to those with whom he works—

To W. Warren Haynes, for his stimulating guidance and his warm friendship.

MARTIN B. SOLOMON JR.

# CONTENTS

# TABLES AND FIGURES

# 1

## INTRODUCTION

$\mathcal{T}$ HERE HAVE been numerous studies of investment, and theoretical tools have been developed for the analysis of investment decisions. Many of these tools emphasize profitability and acceptance criteria and say little about the search for investment alternatives, seemingly taking for granted that the businessman already possesses a number of investment possibilities. Most studies, too, stress the theoretical approach to investments and give comparatively slight attention to the actual behavior of firms in making investment decisions. Because of this emphasis upon the theoretical, perhaps, the practical businessman appears to give little recognition to and make little use of the analytical tools for investment decisions which economic theory has provided him, and, as one economist says, "in general . . . the analysis and appraisal of investment projects is the most backward area of management."[1]

It is especially true that investments in the field of small business have received little analysis, both by the theorist and by the businessman himself. The theorist tends to ignore the small firm. The investment problems of small business are often not of sufficient interest to attract study, while research itself is made difficult by the poor records kept by most small businesses and by the fact that many decisions are made intuitively with the decision maker sometimes unable or unwilling to explain why he acted as he did.

This study of investment decisions in small business aims to fill, at least partially, a neglected area in managerial economics. It discusses the prescriptions which theory has made and points out the assumptions which are involved in them. It compares the methods of the businessman with the prescriptions of theory. Finally, it assesses the usefulness of various theoretical tools for investment analysis within the framework of small business practice, recognizing the limitations imposed by assumptions of theory and the time bind in which the small businessman appears to find himself. The approach involves looking at the theory and then at business behavior as it is revealed in actual cases.

The cases in this study result from intensive interviews with the managers of 40 different firms which were in turn drawn from a total of 88 firms.[2] The criteria used in selecting the firms are those of the Small Business Administration. Most of the companies are single proprietorships or small, family-owned corporations with one or two levels of man-

[1] George Terborgh, *Business Investment Policy* (Washington, D. C.: Machinery and Allied Products Institute and Council for Technological Advancement, 1958), p. 4.

[2] For details on the 88 firms, see W. Warren Haynes, *Pricing Decisions in Small Business* (Lexington: University of Kentucky Press, 1962).

2

agement. Among the 40 are a few larger firms; one manufacturer, for example, employs 200 people while another company has annual sales of $5 to $6 million. In initially selecting the firms no attempt was made to secure a representative group. Lack of willingness on the part of small businessmen would preclude the possibility of obtaining a representative sample of small business no matter how well endowed a research project. Often several companies from the same industry were chosen so that comparisons might be made of their practices. Most of the firms are located within a limited area.

From the beginning it was decided that an unstructured interview would provide the best means of investigating the complexities of decision making. A questionnaire to be completed by the firm's management would likely furnish only superficial answers, and the questionnaire or any other set list of questions might easily fail to reveal important conditions or influences upon management. Interviewers did, however, work from a list of general topics to be covered, but managers were encouraged to talk at length about any investments they were planning or had completed. In particular, decisions currently in progress were made the primary subjects for discussion because at each interview the businessman could reveal his latest thinking. In this way he could not so easily rationalize making poor investments; also, the interviewer was able to note changes in the investor's mood and his methods of analysis at different periods in the decision-making process. One interview would often suggest further questions that could be pursued at later meetings. Other questions were also suggested during discussions of individual cases by the team of interviewers. Most firms, therefore, participated in several sessions, ranging in length from one to four hours; one manager took part in sixteen different interviews.

Only a few of the firms studied were engaged in investment decisions that were significant or that had interesting features. As a result this study discusses only fourteen actual

3

cases. Most of the small firms placed relatively little emphasis on investment planning, and interviews with them produced cases without significance. A few of the latter are discussed as being typical of the majority. While the number of firms investigated in this study is not sufficient to constitute a representative sample of small business practice, the findings based upon them do appear to possess general applicability.

# 2

## CAPITAL BUDGETING—
## AN OVERALL VIEW

*C*APITAL budgeting is that part of financial management which deals with the investment of present funds in exchange for uncertain future returns. The term "investment" includes not only expenditures for buildings and equipment but also any expenditures, such as those for advertising and for research and development, which are expected to yield future returns. Although the term "capital budgeting" in theory may imply an orderly, well-planned, scientific program, in practice the approach to investment decisions is hardly so formal or so orderly. Some managements are unwilling or unable to apply the necessary theory; others are not even aware of its existence.

Capital budgeting might be subdivided into five managerial functions:

(a) continuous and creative searching for investment opportunities;

(b) forecasting the supply and cost of funds for investment purposes;

(c) estimating each project's cash flows and other benefits;

(d) ranking and choosing among competing projects;

(e) postauditing already committed investments.

The importance of each function depends upon the type and size of the firm. Some of these functions are vital in large firms but are not critical in small companies. The reverse is also true. For example, the search function appears extremely important for small firms, but large firms need not devote resources to it. Postauditing is probably not vital in the small concern, but it may be a necessity in the large company. The difference between large and small firms has been essentially ignored in the past.

The continuing and creative search for investment opportunities has until recently received little attention in the literature on management. Most writers give it some space, but since it is difficult to quantify, their discussion is brief and consists of rather obvious generalities. They assume that the businessman has at hand a number of investment possibilities and restrict capital budgeting to the consideration of those possibilities already at hand. If the discovery of investment alternatives is a significant factor in capital budgeting, then the proverbial cart is a mile or two ahead of the horse.

If a businessman can save $1,000 by purchasing a $100 machine, it appears that he should invest. However, if his total available funds consist of only this $100, he might profitably search for a better alternative that returns, say, $2,000 or $3,000 for the same $100 investment.

In our judgment too much attention has been devoted in past literature to choosing among alternatives and too little to discovering them, an emphasis that this volume attempts to counteract.

The forecast of funds available for investment purposes includes those from both external sources (individuals and lending institutions) and internal ones (within the firm itself). Admittedly, forecasting funds may be difficult and uncertain; but some reasonable estimate is usually possible, even if it is relatively crude. An estimate of the additional working capital requirements that might be necessitated by the investment can then be subtracted from the total available internal and external funds. This remainder will approximate the maximum investment funds available in the next period.

Estimating the cost of funds is more complex and, as a result, is the most disputed area of investment theory. What is a firm's cost of capital? Debt and equity capital and internal funds can involve different costs. Dividend yields on equity capital are usually higher than interest payments on debt, and equity financing dilutes control of ownership; however, the comparison of dividends and interest is only one of many factors in calculating the costs of debt and equity financing. Debt financing may be less appealing because of such objectionable features as working capital and dividend restrictions, risks of default, and loss of managerial flexibility. The cost of internal funds is an opportunity cost; that is, funds could be tied up in an investment when they might more advantageously be used in some other way. Some writers advocate simply using the dividend yield as the firm's cost of capital.[1] Others suggest a weighted average of interest and dividend costs.[2] Still others hypothesize that the cost of capital is unaffected by

[1] Milton H. Spencer and Louis Siegelman, *Managerial Economics* (Homewood, Ill.: Richard D. Irwin, 1959).

[2] Harold Bierman, Jr., and Seymour Smidt, *The Capital Budgeting Decision* (New York: Macmillan Co., 1960).

debt.[3] Some argue that comparisons of debt and equity costs are impossible. The Lutzes[4] distinguish between the borrowing rate and the lending rate of interest in measuring the cost of capital; the borrowing rate is what the firm must pay for capital, and the lending rate is that rate at which it can invest (opportunity cost).

The theoretical questions on the supply and cost of capital, while of interest to the scholar, are so complex that there can be serious doubt of their usefulness to the small businessman[5] and, therefore, they are not treated further in this study.

An estimate of the expected cash flows and other benefits is one part of evaluating each prospective investment. The refined methods for ranking investments are discussed fully in the next chapter; they consider such factors as the cash flows for each year of the comparison period, the project life,[6] and the terminal salvage value as well as intangible benefits. Less rigorous methods require estimates of only the first year's income.

The estimate of cash flows or net benefits should include all relevant changes in costs and revenues which will be affected by the decision. The value assigned project life requires that some figure be given for deterioration and obsolescence. Intangible benefits, such as improved morale, safer conditions, etc., are included in the analysis by assessing them at some dollar value. The value of these benefits is

[3] Franco Modigliani and Merton Miller, "The Cost of Capital, Corporation Finance and the Theory of Investment," *American Economic Review*, XLVIII (June 1958), 261-97.

[4] Friedrich and Vera Lutz, *The Theory of Investment of the Firm* (Princeton: Princeton University Press, 1951).

[5] For more discussion, see Ezra Solomon (ed.), *The Management of Corporate Capital* (Glencoe, Ill.: Free Press, 1959), pp. 91-202; Joseph R. Rose, "The Cost of Capital, Corporation Finance, and the Theory of Investment: Comment," *American Economic Review*, XLIX (September 1959), 638-69.

[6] Life is used here to mean actual life and has no necessary relation to accounting life (depreciable life). Estimates of income or saving should be made for the number of years of the longest lived alternative being considered.

subjective, but their exclusion from the analysis may mislead management in determining the full impact and profitability of a proposal.

To prepare reasonable estimates of these factors, management needs to secure information which varies depending on the proposal. Some expensive projects promising huge returns justify extensive research. Others that are obviously highly profitable require little. Similarly, projects whose returns are obviously negligible can be discarded without securing extensive data. Just how management obtains the information for estimating project returns is another neglected area of investment theory.

Ranking and choosing among competing proposals involves establishing some measure or yardstick of profitability and a choice criterion. Theoretically, a firm could construct a graphical representation of the supply schedule of funds that are available at different costs and a demand schedule that reflects all available investment opportunities in terms of what will be called the discounted rate of return (discussed in the next chapter). Such a graph is shown in Figure 2-1.

Suppose that the amounts of money or credit available are plotted against the cost of capital (borrowing rate). Figure 2-1 shows the marginal cost of capital (SS) rising as the amount obtained increases.[7] All available investment opportunities are plotted on the same graph, in the order of their returns (yields). The resultant is a marginal demand schedule for funds (DD), as shown in Figure 2-1. All investments with yields above the intersection of the two curves should be undertaken—they are profitable. The point of indifference is at the intersection of the two curves. For

[7] The slope depicted in the supply of funds schedule is controversial. Some scholars might revolt at the lack of perfect elasticity, but surely there is some slope when the schedule includes subjective costs. If one is willing to admit that firms prefer internal financing to external financing, there should be no argument against the upward slope. Since internal funds are limited and firms avoid external financing, some point on the curve must be higher than some other.

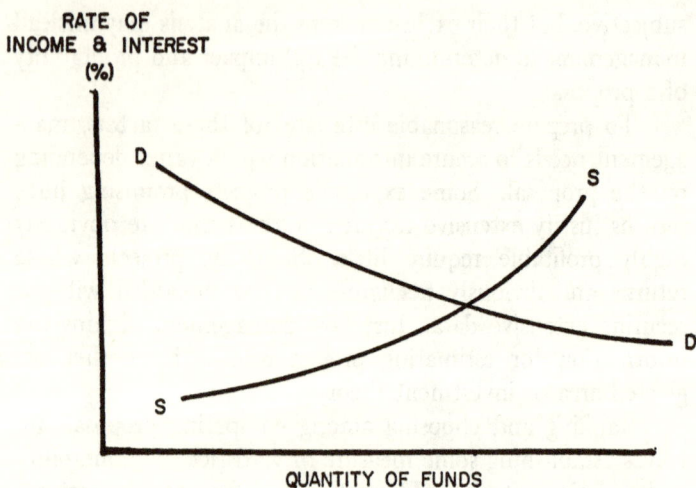

FIGURE 2-1
SUPPLY AND DEMAND FOR FUNDS

amounts above the intersection, the cost of capital is greater than the yield and a loss on this excess results. Below, an opportunity loss occurs from not investing more. But so many uncertainties exist that for all practical purposes such a graph is impractical.

Evaluation of investment proposals involves longrun considerations. How does a proposal fit into longrun plans? Some projects might seem profitable, but if they are opposed to the company's longrun goals, added costs result. The purchase of a profitable company whose reputation is questionable might be a detriment to the purchasing company's image.

In addition, working capital requirements must be taken into consideration. How will the pending proposals affect working capital? If they are accepted, will adequate funds be available for current requirements? Will adequate resources be available to take advantage of future profitable opportunities that might arise? These are all difficult questions that bear upon the decision. "Because today's capital ex-

10

penditures make the bed that the company must lie in tomorrow, today's decisions must be based on definite assumptions as to what tomorrow will be like."[8]

Postauditing investment projects is important for comparing the actual results with the estimates. Careful postaudits can reveal the abilities and shortcomings of personnel responsible for investment decisions. Optimists may estimate greater savings than are actually possible, and pessimists are likely to underestimate profitability. Since postaudits necessitate records of estimates, they therefore contribute to an organized decision-making process.

Many important functions of capital budgeting have been completely ignored in this chapter. For example, authorization and responsibility for making investment outlays, organizational considerations, administrative procedures, education and training have not been discussed here; some of these functions are considered later as they relate to the actual case studies.

[8] Joel Dean, "Measuring the Productivity of Capital," *Harvard Business Review*, XXXII (January-February 1954), 120-30.

*3*

# CAPITAL RATIONING FORMULAS—
# THEORETICALLY CORRECT METHODS

𝒯*HE MOST* technical analysis in the current literature on investment is devoted to choosing among competing investment proposals. Many economists have given serious attention to the problem of profitability and acceptance criteria.[1] Since this function of capital budgeting lends itself to quantification, formulas have been most popular in the literature. This chapter reviews two methods for calculating profitability which have been accepted as theoretically sound —present value analysis and discounted rate of return analysis. Not only will the discussion serve to introduce some of the factors which need to be considered in comparing future profits, but the methods themselves offer a standard against which actual business practice can be compared.

## PRESENT VALUE ANALYSIS

*Associated* with any investment is a stream of expected cash inflows and outflows. A dollar received next year is less valuable than a dollar received today because it could accumulate interest between now and next year. But differing income streams make the comparison of two or more investments difficult. Present value analysis, which is generally considered to be the theoretically correct or best method for evaluating and ranking investments,[2] normalizes future cash flows by discounting them at some rate of interest. In other words, the "present value" of an investment, as established by this method, is a cash lump sum today that is equivalent to a stream of future returns. When two investment proposals differ in life and pattern of future returns, the standard method of comparison is present value which discounts all of these future returns so that the cash lump sums can be compared. The general formula for present value is[3]

$$V = \frac{Q_1}{(1+r)} + \frac{Q_2}{(1+r)^2} + \cdots + \frac{Q_n}{(1+r)^n}$$
$$+ \frac{S}{(1+r)^n} - C \quad (1)$$

[1] The leaders have been Friedrich and Vera Lutz; Joel Dean, *Capital Budgeting* (New York: Columbia University Press, 1951); George Terborgh, *Dynamic Equipment Policy* (New York: McGraw-Hill Book Co., 1949).

[2] See Ezra Solomon, "The Arithmetic of Capital Budgeting Decisions," *Journal of Business*, XXIX (April 1956), 124-29; J. H. Lorie and L. J. Savage, "Three Problems in Capital Rationing," *Journal of Business*, XXVIII (October 1955), 229-39; Bierman and Smidt.

[3] For compatibility with other formulas, we define present value in terms of excess present value (present value minus the cost of the investment proposal).

where $V$ = excess present value over cost,
$Q_t$ = posttax cash flow in year $t$ (where $t$ is 1, 2, 3, ... $n$)
$S$ = terminal salvage value,
$r$ = rate of interest,
$C$ = cost of asset,
$n$ = useful life of asset.

Consider a machine selling for $4,000. Suppose that an interest rate of 20 percent is used to discount the stream of incomes or savings: $1,000 one year from now, $2,000 two years from now, and $4,500 three years from now. The terminal salvage value is $500 at the end of three years.

The excess present value is

$$V = \frac{\$1,000}{(1+.20)} + \frac{\$2,000}{(1+.20)^2} + \frac{\$4,500 + \$500}{(1+.20)^3} - \$4,000$$

$$V = \$833.33 + \$1,388.89 + \$2,893.50 - \$4,000$$

$$V = \$1,115.72$$

The present value can be interpreted as follows: if the annual earnings are reinvested at 20 percent interest,[4] this stream of cash flows ($1,000, $2,000, $5,000) would amount to $8,840 at the end of three years. The present value of $8,840 received three years from now is $5,115.72. The excess present value over cost equals $1,115.72 ($5,115.72 − $4,000).

*Rate of interest*

The discounting rate used in present value analysis is the lending rate (the rate of interest that the firm can obtain in the loan market or in some other enterprise).[5] The lending rate is a measure of opportunity cost in investments with similar degrees of risk. If the lending rate is less than the borrowing rate, then the latter is applicable. If a firm can obtain a 20 percent return elsewhere, it would

[4] In this example, interest is compounded annually. Reinvestment takes place at the end of each year.
[5] H. V. Roberts, "Current Problems in the Economics of Capital Budgeting," *Journal of Business*, XXX (January 1957), 12-16.

be foolish (generally) to invest in a project that yields only 15 percent (assuming the same degree of risk). If one discounts the expected cash flows from an investment yielding a 15 percent return at 20 percent, a present value less than the supply price results. The excess present value is negative and hence the project is rejected.

*Comparing two investments*

When the acquisition costs of investments are different, one needs to compute present value as a percentage of original cost in order to rank projects in order of profitability.[6] The investments that maximize present value per dollar of outlay are the most profitable.[7] If the acquisition costs are the same, the present values can be directly compared. Assume that an alternative proposal to that previously mentioned is one that produces $4,000 the first year, $2,000 the second year and $500 the third year. Again the cost is $4,000 and the salvage value is $500 after the third year. This comparison involves identical supply prices, so that the present values can be compared directly. Discounted at 20 percent, the present value of this stream of cash flows is $5,300.90. Thus the excess of present value over cost is $1,300.90 ($5,300.90 — $4,000 = $1,300.90). In other words this second investment proposal is more profitable than the first. A comparison of these two examples points out the fallacy in employing average annual returns as a guide to decisions. The average annual returns (exclusive of reinvestment opportunities) are $2,666 for the first proposal and $2,333 for the second. In this case the time pattern of the revenue stream causes the second proposal to be more profitable even though its average annual returns are less.

[6] The implicit assumption here is that net cash outlays occur only at the time of the asset's acquisition.

[7] There is not general agreement on this very technical subject. See Lutz, pp. 16-48; Clifford G. Hildreth, "Note on Maximization Criteria," *Quarterly Journal of Economics*, LXI (November 1946), 156-64; and Dean, *Harvard Business Review*, XXXII, 120-30.

*Assumptions*

The implicit assumption of present value analysis is that all cash flows are reinvested at the discounting rate of interest. Since the lending rate is the measure of returns on reinvestments, it is appropriate for discounting purposes. If this basic assumption is violated, then present value does not correctly normalize future cash flows.

The computation of present value requires that depreciation and interest charges are not deducted from savings or revenue. We are concerned with cash flows from an investment, and depreciation expense is not a cash flow. Interest expense is implicit in the discounting process. If present value is greater than the acquisition cost, the asset will pay for itself and return more than the discounting rate of interest. If present value is equal to the acquisition cost, then the investment will pay for itself and yield exactly the discounting rate of interest.

## DISCOUNTED RATE OF RETURN

*The discounted* rate of return is a concept closely related to present value. It too transforms future incomes into today's values but in the form of a percentage rather than a dollar amount. In essence, it tells us the highest rate of interest (cost of capital) that is compatible with profitability. It is the rate of interest that when applied as a discounting rate equates the stream of cash inflows and outflows; that is

$$C = \frac{Q_1}{(1+r)} + \frac{Q_2}{(1+r)^2} + \cdots + \frac{Q_n + S}{(1+r)^n} \qquad (2)$$

The only unknown in equation (2) is $r$, the discounting rate of interest; $Q_t$, $S$, $n$ and $C$ are all assumed to be known. The practical solution involves trial and error methods. The first example cited returned $1,000, $2,000, and $5,000 in each of three years. If the acquisition cost of the asset were $4,230, the resulting discounted rate of return is approximately 30 percent.

$$\$4,230 = \frac{\$1,000}{(1.30)} + \frac{\$2,000}{(1.30)^2} + \frac{\$5,000}{(1.30)^3}$$

An $r$ of 30 percent satisfies the equality; hence it is the discounted rate of return. The implicit assumption here is that the funds are reinvested at the *resultant* rate of interest. If the discounted rate of return is greater than the cost of capital (lending rate), the investment is profitable. Generally, it is possible to rank investments by their discounted rates of return and to prefer projects with the highest rates. When projects differ in length of life, difficulties may arise in the interpretation of the discounted rates of return; a discussion of this problem follows.[8]

## APPARENT INCONSISTENCY BETWEEN THE TWO METHODS OF ANALYSIS

*If one* desires only to determine whether a single investment proposal is profitable, the discounted rate of return and present value analysis perform consistently; whenever excess present value is positive, the discounted rate of return is greater than the cost of capital. Whenever excess present value is negative, the discounted rate of return is less than the cost of capital. However, when a ranking of investment proposals is desired, the two methods can sometimes conflict.

George Terborgh has shown, for example, that four investment proposals can be given opposite rankings by the two approaches.[9] Four investment proposals (A, B, C, and D) promise annual earnings of $1,000 per year for 5, 10, 15, and 20 years respectively. Their discounted rates of return are 20, 18, 17, and 16 percent respectively; therefore the order of preference is A, B, C, D. When excess present

[8] If used for ranking investments, a poor ranking might result due to factors other than differences in the length of life of proposals under consideration. See Bierman and Smidt, pp. 34-46.

[9] George Terborgh, "Some Comments on the Dean-Smith Article on the MAPI Formula," *Journal of Business*, XXIX (April 1956), 138-40.

value as a percentage of investment outlay is computed, an opposite ranking results (assuming a 10 percent cost of capital). According to the excess present value criterion, the order of profitability is D, C, B, A. The figures are shown below.

| Invest- ment proposal | Length of life (years) | Amount of investment (cost) | Present value @ 10% | Excess present value as % of cost | Discounted rate of return |
|---|---|---|---|---|---|
| A | 5 | $2,991 | $3,791 | 26.8 | 20 |
| B | 10 | 4,494 | 6,145 | 36.7 | 18 |
| C | 15 | 5,324 | 7,606 | 42.9 | 17 |
| D | 20 | 5,929 | 8,514 | 43.6 | 16 |

The inconsistency in ranking results from differences in assumptions of the two methods.[10] When lives of the investment proposals differ, both methods give results that are questionable on a purely theoretical basis. The discounted rate of return assumes that proceeds are reinvested at the resultant rate of return. We cannot reasonably assume this;

[10] The ranking inconsistency found in the two methods can be reconciled if the reinvestment rate is made explicit in formulating the discounted rate of return. To accomplish this, one would compound the annual proceeds to the final year of comparison at the reinvestment rate of interest and then compute the discounted rate of return for the accumulated amount in the last year. To illustrate, the five-year investment (proposal A) is analyzed. The comparison period is 20 years, the life of the longest lived proposal. Since the reinvestment rate is 10 percent, the annual proceeds of proposal A ($1,000 for five years) are compounded at 10 percent interest to the end of year 20. The accumulated cash is $25,503 at that time. The discounted rate of return on $25,503 received 20 years in the future is 11.4 percent. In the form of an equation this is

$$\frac{\sum_{t=15}^{19} (\$1,000)(1.10)^t}{(1+r)^{20}} = \$2,991$$

where an $r$ of .114 satisfies the equality. If this procedure is used for all four investment proposals, the resulting discounted rates of return for proposals A, B, C, and D are 11.4, 11.8, 12.0 and 12.1 percent respectively. This modified ranking is consistent with the excess present value ranking. See Solomon, *Journal of Business*, XXIX, 126.

if proceeds are reinvested at the resultant rate, it is purely fortuitous.

On the other hand, present value analysis is not free from pitfalls. It assumes that the reinvestment rate and the discounting rate are identical for all future annual proceeds (cash flows) within the comparative time period. Since this assumption ignores investment proposals that might occur in the future, it becomes a source of possible error. Even when the discounting rate accurately reflects the reinvestment opportunities, difficulties may exist. If project lives differ, then some explicit assumptions about the reinvestment of entire projects are necessary for theoretical correctness in the ranking process.

While the present value method of ranking investments is often considered the best under rigid assumptions, in practice it is subject to errors that destroy its superiority. As Lorie and Savage suggest,[11] for the vast majority of actual investments it is likely that the discounted rate of return and the present value methods will rank investment proposals similarly. Throughout the remainder of this volume both methods will be called theoretically correct, although no method—in practice—is theoretically correct. Nevertheless, because these two formulations consider the time value of money and the entire length of a project's life, they are the best methods available; they will both be used as criteria for accuracy when evaluating other measures of profitability.

[11] Lorie and Savage, p. 238.

19

# 4

# CAPITAL RATIONING FORMULAS—
# ALTERNATIVE METHODS

*THE DISCOUNTED* rate of return and present value methods are cumbersome and time consuming; alternative methods simplify the process of investment evaluation. The simplification of complex factors naturally reduces accuracy. Each of the alternative methods mentioned here fails to consider some of the factors such as the lower value of future income and various lengths of project life. Time can be an important consideration, but it also creates difficulties in ranking.

The extreme uncertainty involved in many actual investment decisions may nullify the advantages of refined methods of analysis. Refined formulas require a forecast of incremental costs and revenues for each relevant future period. Uncertainty discourages some entrepreneurs from applying refined techniques; for them, an alternative method of analysis is welcome. To others who have no knowledge of the theoretical measures, alternative methods seem the only practical and sensible approach.

## FORMULAS FOR INVESTMENT EVALUATION

*This* chapter compares the accuracy of alternative rationing formulas with present value and the discounted rate of return under conditions of certainty in cost and revenue forecasts. A later chapter concerns itself with uncertainty. First we shall reformulate the discounted rate of return so that it is more easily compared with some alternative formulas.

The discounted rate of return is the rate of interest $(r)$ that satisfies the equation[1]

$$C = \frac{Q_1}{(1+r)} + \frac{Q_2}{(1+r)^2} + \cdots + \frac{Q_n + S}{(1+r)^n} \qquad (1)$$

where $Q_t$ = posttax cash flows[2] in year $t$,
$n$ = useful life of the asset in years,
$S$ = terminal salvage value of the asset,
$C$ = cost of proposal or net investment.

If each annual cash inflow $(Q_t)$ is the same and the salvage value's present value is negligible, equation (1) reduces to

$$C = \sum_{t=1}^{n} \frac{Q}{(1+r)^t} \qquad (2)$$

which is the same as[3]

[1] Net cash outflows occur only at the time of asset acquisition.
[2] Essentially this is posttax profit plus depreciation expense and interest expense. Some authors suggest that interest expense be considered only in the cost of capital. Bierman and Smidt, p. 97.
[3] See Spencer and Siegelman, p. 388.

21

$$C = \frac{Q}{r} - \frac{Q}{r}\left(\frac{1}{1+r}\right)^n \qquad (3)$$

Transposing, we get

$$r = \frac{Q}{C} - \frac{Q}{C} \cdot \left(\frac{1}{1+r}\right)^n \qquad (4)$$

Equation (4) is useful in comparing the discounted rate of return with alternative methods.

*Payback period*

In practice, the payback period is the most commonly used investment profitability criterion.[4] The formula for the payback period is

$$\text{Payback period} = C/Q \qquad (5)$$

where $C$ = cost of proposal or net investment,
   $Q$ = net posttax cash flow.

Consider an example. A new high-speed lathe's cost is $9,000. It will save $3,860 per year if purchased. No increased revenue is foreseen. If depreciated on a straight line basis for nine years, annual depreciation expense amounts to $1,000. $Q$, the posttax cash flow, can be generalized as[5]

$$Q = D + (R - D)(1 - X)$$

where $D$ = annual accounting depreciation expense,
   $R$ = annual increased revenue and/or decreased cost,
   $X$ = tax rate.

If the tax rate is 30 percent, $Q$ in the example is

$$\$1,000 + (\$3,860 - \$1,000)(1 - .30) = \$3,002$$

[4] The discussion follows that in Myron J. Gordon, "The Payoff Period and the Rate of Profit," *Journal of Business*, XXVIII (October 1955), 253-60.

[5] This form is appropriate if the firm is making profits, and only when a single tax rate is applicable. Interest expense is ignored. In a strict sense, this formula does not necessarily represent cash flow but rather is an approximation.

or about $3,000. The payback period then equals $9,000/$3,000, or three years.

The payback period fails to consider the length of the investment's life and the time value of money. Its indiscriminate use can lead to decisions favoring less profitable investments. For example, suppose that two proposals are being considered. Proposal A will return an annual posttax cash flow of $5,000 for five years. Proposal B will return an annual posttax cash flow of $4,000 for 15 years. Each proposal costs $10,000. Using the payback period, one would choose proposal A because the payback period is two years while for B it is two and one-half years; but B is more profitable.

The effect of using the payback period appears to be the conservation of cash rather than securing the greatest profits. In a rather crude way it indicates the length of time required for recovery of the original investment. When an investment is particularly risky or subject to a high rate of obsolescence, a fast return may be the most important consideration. A company, saddled with acute shortages of funds, may prefer a faster return of original investment to greater profitability. A speedy return of investment and a high profitability are both important considerations; when risk increases, so does the importance of a rapid payback; but a short payback is not necessarily consistent with high profitability.

*Payback reciprocal*

The payback reciprocal is merely the inverse of the payback period. If the payback period is five years, the reciprocal is 1/5 or 20 percent. The payback reciprocal is an estimate of the maximum possible discounted rate of return on an investment, given equal annual returns and negligible salvage value. The payback reciprocal contains the same information as the payback period. It facilitates comparison with the discounted rate of return. The payback reciprocal is given by

$$PR = Q/C \tag{6}$$

where $Q$ = posttax cash flow,[6]

$C$ = cost of the asset or net investment.

A comparison of the payback reciprocal with the discounted rate of return reveals a similarity.

$$r = \frac{Q}{C} - \frac{Q}{C} \left(\frac{1}{1+r}\right)^n \tag{4}$$

$$PR = Q/C \tag{6}$$

As $n$ (the life of the project) increases, the second term in equation (4) diminishes, and the equation approximates that for the payback reciprocal. If $n$ is infinite, these equations do in fact become equal. For small $n$, equations (4) and (6) diverge.

Another method of formulating the payback reciprocal is the pretax payback reciprocal multiplied by one minus the tax rate; this is the *simple* payback reciprocal.

### Rate of income on average investment

Rate of income on average investment is sometimes called the accounting rate of return or the financial statement method. There are many variations of rate of return; all (except the discounted rate of return) are a ratio of receipts to cost. Two such "rates of return" are discussed. The first utilizes net posttax cash flows *minus* depreciation divided by average investment. Average investment is defined as cost of the investment (net investment) divided by two[7] or

Average investment $= C/Q$

[6] Two different methods of computing $Q$ are: (a) first-year performance and (b) average annual returns; both are more fully explained later.

[7] If salvage value is considered, average investment is generally formulated as cost plus salvage value divided by two. This feature confuses analysis because larger salvage values produce lower rates of income.

Average investment is the denominator in this "accountant's rate of return." The numerator is $Q - D = Q - C/n$ or cash flow minus depreciation, where $D$ is annual depreciation expense. Therefore, rate of income on average investment (AR) is shown as[8]

$$AR = \frac{Q - C/n}{C/2} = \frac{2Q}{C} - \frac{2}{n} \qquad (7)$$

where $Q =$ posttax cash flow,
$\quad\ \ C =$ cost of the asset (net investment),
$\quad\ \ n =$ useful life.

Here, as $n$ becomes very large, the rate of income on average investment approaches twice the discounted rate of return and twice the payback reciprocal. For small $n$, it is a better estimate of the discounted rate of return than the payback reciprocal.[9] (See Figure 4-2.) AR is always greater than $r$ (actual discounted rate of return), given equal annual returns, and negligible salvage value.

*Rate of income on total investment*

Rate of income on total investment is similar to equation (7) except that total investment is used in the denominator. It is given by

$$TR = Q/C - 1/n \qquad (8)$$

In this case, as $n$ becomes large, rate of income on total investment becomes a closer estimate of the discounted rate of return. $TR$ is always less than the actual (discounted) rate of return, given that the annual returns are equal. In using the accounting rate of return, $Q$ is usually taken as first year performance. It can also be formulated as average annual returns.

[8] This formulation assumes that the accountant depreciates the asset equally over the useful life. Perhaps a more realistic approach is to depreciate the asset in particular number of years, say, five.
[9] Gordon, pp. 253-60.

## The MAPI system

The MAPI system,[10] developed by the Machinery and Allied Products Institute for the systematic analysis of investments, is essentially a rate of return concept, except that it compares investing in a project or going without it for *one more year*. A version of the system, published in 1958, is more flexible; it explicitly considers taxes and accelerated depreciation, if desired. Although the MAPI system is primarily designed for determining whether to replace machinery, it can be used as a general rationing device. The MAPI system takes deterioration and obsolescence into account. It assumes that as an asset ages, its efficiency declines and it becomes more obsolete because of new technological advances. The MAPI rate of return, $MR$, may be summarized as

$$MR = \frac{(R_1 + Y)(1 - X) - (Z - TX)}{C} \qquad (9)$$

where $R_1 =$ net next year's pretax operating advantage of the proposal,

$\quad\ Y\ =$ loss of salvage value that existing project will incur during the next year, plus capital additions planned for the existing project next year (pretax),

$\quad X\ =$ tax rate,

$\quad Z\ =$ next year's capital consumption of the proposal,

$\quad T =$ next year's tax deductions on the new project,

$\quad C\ =$ net investment required.

The consideration of next year's capital consumption is the feature that distinguishes MAPI from other methods of analysis. Essentially it is the difference between the present value (based on the discounted rate of return) before and after the first year. Published charts provide estimates of capital consumption adjusted for taxes. Figure 4-1 is one of

[10] Terborgh, *Business Investment Policy*.

26

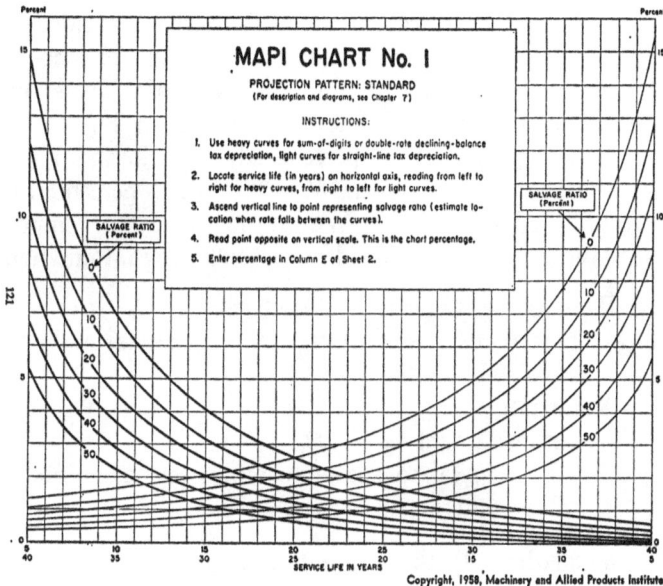

**MAPI CHART No. I**

PROJECTION PATTERN: STANDARD
(For description and diagrams, see Chapter 7)

INSTRUCTIONS:

1. Use heavy curves for sum-of-digits or double-rate declining-balance tax depreciation, light curves for straight-line tax depreciation.

2. Locate service life (in years) on horizontal axis, reading from left to right for heavy curves, from right to left for light curves.

3. Ascend vertical line to point representing salvage ratio (estimate location when rate falls between the curves).

4. Read point opposite on vertical scale. This is the chart percentage.

5. Enter percentage in Column E of Sheet 2.

Copyright, 1958, Machinery and Allied Products Institute

FIGURE 4-1
MAPI CHART No. 1

three charts available. It assumes a linear decline in operating advantage over the life of the project—a constant rate of deterioration and obsolescence. An example illustrates the use of the MAPI system.

Suppose that a fleet owner is considering a truck replacement. The old truck is ready for an engine overhaul, a cost of $200. Prorated over, say, three years, the first year cost is $67. Operating advantage next year is estimated to be $700; an added $600 in revenue due to the increased capacity of the truck and a reduced $100 in the cost of gas, oil, and repairs, other than the overhaul. The old truck can be sold now for $400; one year hence it will be worth only $300; so $100 is saved by selling the truck now. Assume a 50 percent tax rate. The new truck costs $3,000, will last five years, and will be worth 20 percent of its cost or $600 at the end of five years. The net investment is $3,000 minus $400 salvage

27

value of the old truck minus $200 overhaul avoided or $2,400. The firm uses straight line depreciation for accounting purposes. Capital consumption minus the tax saving due to depreciation and interest is found in Figure 4-1. Using the light curves, 20 percent salvage ratio and a five-year life, the chart shows that $Z - TX = 10.8$ percent; 10.8 percent of $3,000 = $324. We are now ready to compute the MAPI rate of return, based on the following information:

$R_1$, next year's operating advantage = $700,

Y, next year's loss of salvage value + capital additions avoided = $167,

X, tax rate = .50,

C, net investment = $2,400,

$Z - TX$, capital consumption minus tax saving due to depreciation and interest = $324.

From equation (9), the MAPI rate of return is

$$MR = \frac{(\$700 + \$167)(.50) - \$324}{\$2,400} = \frac{\$110}{\$2,400} = 4.6\%$$

The MAPI system has been developed to provide a relatively simple approximation to the theoretically correct measures of profitability and rank. Its accuracy will be compared with that of other methods later in this chapter.

*Completely qualitative methods*

Profitability calculations do not enter into all investment decisions. For example, parts are often replaced because of "necessity." It would be foolish to go through a complete analysis every time a part needs replacing or a machine needs minor repairs. It may be equally foolish to decide on building a new plant in the same subjective manner that we replace a part. Necessity and urgency commonly describe projects that have gained favor. When they are used as investment criteria, the most persuasive or clever sponsor may receive a disproportionate share of resources. Urgency may or may not be a sound criterion. A machine may need a new part costing only a few dollars, but replacing a thousand parts failing separately becomes a sizable investment. It may be better to replace a machine than to put thousands of dollars into new parts or repairs a few dollars at a time.

Postponability is another qualitative criterion; if possible, an investment is pushed into the future. Major expansion and modernization may usually be postponed. But, as Joel Dean states: "The use of postponability as a criterion is likely to result in a stagnant operation."[11]

On the one hand, postponability, urgency, and necessity may lead to comparatively unprofitable investment decisions. On the other, in view of the uncertainty of the future, the theoretical criteria provide no guarantee of maximum returns.

*Maximum returns versus adequate returns*

Our interviews seem to indicate that few businessmen think in terms of "optimal" or "best" problem solutions: they focus attention on "good" or "satisfactory" solutions. Herbert Simon, William Baumol, and others have developed theories that recognize this fact. Their empirical studies and ours tend to support the theory that businessmen do not maximize profits or returns on investment; maximization involves the simultaneous analysis of too many complicated variables with uncertain and unpredictable interrelationships. As an escape from this confusion, the businessman searches for acceptable rather than the best solutions to his problems.

Analyzing the complicated variables of business decisions has been rendered easier by the development of electronic computers. Complex interrelationships can sometimes be programed and analyzed using computers. This, however, does not relieve men of decision-making responsibility, but it does facilitate more intelligent decisions. The severest limitation in the analysis of business problems is uncertainty; coping with it requires judgment. Even a computer must be

[11] Joel Dean, *Managerial Economics* (New York: Prentice-Hall, 1951), p. 567.

programed by humans using judgment; the resulting analysis is no better than the judgments of these same people. Although a computer performs arithmetic operations faster and more accurately than a man, it cannot eliminate uncertainty about the future. It can only find the best solutions within a framework of reference set forth by its program. This frame of reference is necessarily limited in the number of variables and relationships, and therefore it does not conform to the reality faced by man. If a computer— which can do in a day what would take a man several lifetimes—cannot maximize, neither can men.

As is illustrated in some cases to follow, a vast number of business decisions must be made with limited information about the future. When this is the case, qualitative or alternative methods may be just as useful as any others. More perfect information can lead closer to maximization, but added information involves added costs. The question is whether the additional information is worthwhile in view of its extra costs and its uncertain validity.

In the final analysis, qualitative methods may merit a greater place in investment decisions than past literature has been willing to admit. They may often furnish a reasonable compromise in a complex, uncertain world.

## SOME ANALYTICAL COMPARISONS

*This* section compares some common alternative measures of profitability[12] with theoretical measures. If any of the alternative measures are close estimates of the theoretical formulas, then the additional complexity and refinement of present value or discounted rate of return may not be warranted. There is another reason for the comparisons that follow. Since many small businessmen use alternative measures, a more complete understanding of the relationships

12 These are (a) payback reciprocal, (b) rate of income on average investment, (c) rate of income on total investment, (d) MAPI rate of return. They are alternative to the theoretically correct measures.

between these measures and rigorous formulations will enable us to judge actual business practice more knowledgeably.

At this point we review some of the formulas stated earlier in this chapter. *Salvage value is disregarded in the discussion that follows,* and the formulas are accordingly restated. First the symbols are defined.

$C$ = cost of the asset (net investment required),
$D$ = annual depreciation expense,
$n$ = useful life of the proposal,
$Q$ = posttax cash flow per year,
$Q_t$ = posttax cash flow in year $t$,
$R_t$ = net pretax increased revenues and/or decreased costs in year $t$,
$r$ = rate of interest,
$t$ = time,
$T$ = first year tax deductions on the new project due to depreciation and interest,
$X$ = tax rate,
$Z$ = next year capital consumption of the project.

The posttax cash flow, $Q$, deserves special attention. When $Q$ is used with a subscript, for example, $Q_2$, it stands for the posttax cash flow in the year that is subscripted (in the example year 2) and is computed as follows: $Q_t = (R_t - D)(1 - X) + D$. When $Q$ is used without a subscript, it usually means that the posttax cash flow is the same in each year of the project. If this is not the case, $Q$ can be computed in at least two ways. (1) Using $R_a$ for average pretax income over the life of the project, $Q = (R_a - D)(1 - X) + D$. This is called average annual returns. (2) Using $R_1$ for pretax income in year 1, $Q = (R_1 - D)(1 - X) + D$. This is called first year performance.

Next the eight formulas used in the analysis that follows are presented.

Discounted rate of return is the value of $r$ that satisfies the equality

$$C = \frac{Q_1}{(1+r)} + \frac{Q_2}{(1+r)^2} + \cdots + \frac{Q_n}{(1+r)^n} \qquad (1)$$

Payback reciprocal using first year performance is defined as

$$FPR = \frac{(R_1 - D)(1-X) + D}{C} \qquad (10)$$

Payback reciprocal using average annual returns is defined as

$$APR = \frac{FPR_1 + FPR_2 + \cdots + FPR_n}{n} \qquad (11)$$

Simple payback reciprocal is defined as[18]

$$SPR = \frac{R_1}{C}(1-X) \qquad (12)$$

Rate of income on total investment using first year performance is defined as

$$FTR = \frac{(R_1 - D)(1-X)}{C} \qquad (13)$$

Rate of income on total investment using average annual returns is defined as

$$ATR = \frac{FTR_1 + FTR_2 + \cdots + FTR_n}{n} \qquad (14)$$

Rate of income on average investment is two times equation (13) or (14) depending upon how $Q$ is computed. For purpose of simplicity it is formulated in a general form as

$$AR = 2Q/C - 2/n \qquad (7)$$

MAPI rate of return, disregarding salvage values, is defined as

$$MR = \frac{R_i(1-X) - (Z - TX)}{C} \qquad (9)$$

[18] It is important to realize that while the simple payback reciprocal uses the first year's pretax income in its numerator, this is different from the payback reciprocal using first-year performance. The latter is formulated in (10) while the former is formulated in (12).

Four comparisons follow. The first three compare the alternative methods with the discounted rate of return. The fourth compares the ability of the various alternative rationing methods to rank 12 hypothetical investment proposals.

*Comparison A—accuracy of alternative measures relative to length of life of an investment—constant annual returns*

We assume that an investment yields $1,300 (before taxes) each year for $n$ years. We let $n$ vary from 4 to 20, computing the alternative measures and the discounted rate of return for each $n$: 4, 5, 6, ..., 20. In other words, if $n = 4$, the investment yields $1,300 annual pretax income for four years. If $n = 10$, the investment yields $1,300 per year for ten years. Formulas (1), (7), (9), (10), (12), and (13) are used in the comparison. First we let $n = 4$. Then we compute the different values of the six formulas and plot them. Next we let $n = 5$, compute and plot. This process is continued for $n$ between 4 and 20 inclusive. (Starting at $n = 4$ rather than $n = 1$ avoids the negative answers.) We assume that the asset costs $4,000, that it has no salvage value at $n$, and that the applicable tax rate is 32 percent. We use straight line depreciation for tax purposes.

$Q$ (annual posttax cash flow) is different for each value of $n$ because the annual depreciation expense changes as $n$ changes and affects the tax flow. When $n = 5$, $Q$ is $1,140. When $n = 20$, $Q$ is $948. The only independent variable is $n$, since $C$ is fixed at $4,000 and $R_t$ at $1,300. Figure 4-2 (based on Gordon)[14] shows the relationship between the five alternative measures and the discounted rate of return. Usable life of the investment $(n)$ is plotted along the horizontal axis, and percentage returns (results of the formula calculations) are plotted on the vertical axis.

[14] Gordon. Although the idea for the analysis came from Gordon, his formulations omitted the MAPI rate of return. Also, Gordon was concerned only with constant annual returns; we also investigate the case of declining annual returns. Another difference lies in the various types of payback reciprocals and rates of income that are formulated here.

33

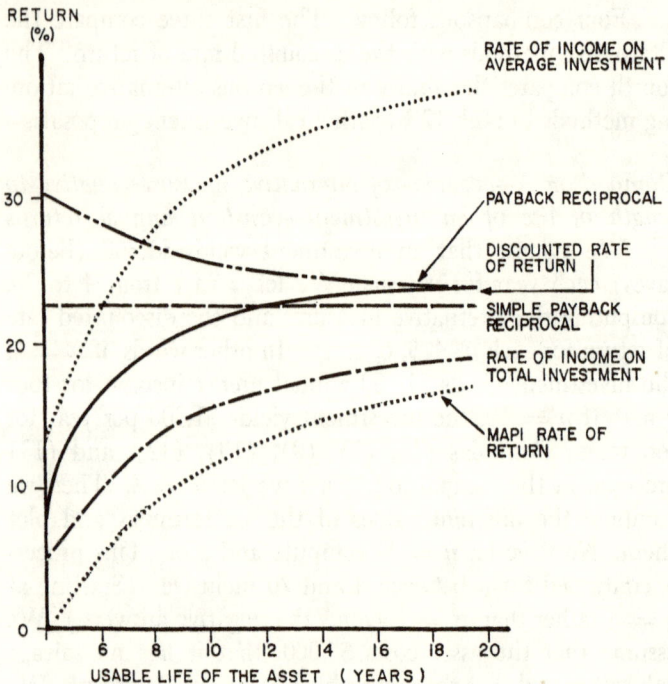

RETURN
(%)

RATE OF INCOME ON
AVERAGE INVESTMENT

30

PAYBACK RECIPROCAL

DISCOUNTED RATE
OF RETURN

SIMPLE PAYBACK
RECIPROCAL

20

RATE OF INCOME ON
TOTAL INVESTMENT

MAPI RATE OF
RETURN

10

0

6   8   10   12   14   16   18.   20
USABLE LIFE OF THE ASSET   ( YEARS )

FIGURE 4-2

Comparison between Discounted Rate of Return and
Alternative Methods—an Asset with Constant Annual
Pretax Returns

The alternative methods are now individually discussed.

1. *Payback reciprocal.* For large values of $n$ both
formulations of the payback reciprocal are excellent estimates
of the discounted rate of return where the same pretax
return is expected year after year. When the life of an
investment with constant returns is short in relation to the
payback period, the payback reciprocal is a poor estimator
of the discounted rate of return. At $n = 20$, the payback
reciprocal and the discounted rate of return are within one

34

percentage point of each other, while at $n = 8$ there is a difference of about 12 percentage points.

2. *MAPI and rate of income on total investment.* Both the MAPI rate of return and rate of income on total investment become better estimates of the discounted rate of return as $n$ increases.[15] Figure 4-2 shows that the discounted rate of return is consistently four to five percentage points greater than the rate of income on total investment for all $n$ and five to eight percentage points greater than the MAPI rate of return for all $n$. It is significant that an almost constant bias exists in the MAPI rate of return and rate of income on total investment when compared to the discounted rate of return.[16] If a businessman uses one of these measures for evaluating investment proposals, he can consider this constant downward bias in his analysis. Even if he does not realize that such a relationship exists, his relative results may be consistent with discounted rate of return analysis.

3. *Rate of income on average investment.* Rate of income on average investment is a better estimate of the discounted rate of return for small values of $n$ but becomes quite inaccurate for large values of $n$. It approaches twice the discounted rate of return.

Figure 4-2 compares the discounted rate of return and alternative methods only for specific values of $n$ and therefore only vertical comparisons are significant.[17]

[15] See Gordon.

[16] The downward bias in the MAPI rate of return as compared with the discounted rate of return results from a difference in the period of analysis. The former measure considers only one year while the latter considers the whole life of the asset.

[17] The reason for this is that the investment proposals for an $n$ of 4 are quite different from those for an $n$ of 5 or 6, since they provide revenues for a longer period of time. Most of the curves on Figure 4-3 rise to the right simply because longer periods of revenue are earned by the proposals with larger $n$'s. This is not true for the payback reciprocal, which ignores length of life. It would be meaningless to say that in Figure 4-3 the MAPI rate of return at $n = 20$ is greater than the discounted rate of return at $n = 5$. This is not the purpose of the diagram.

*Comparison B—accuracy of alternative measures relative to length of life of the investment—declining annual returns*

This example considers investments with continually declining annual pretax returns instead of constant returns. The situation is more realistic: obsolescence or deterioration or both could be responsible for declining returns. Instead of assuming that an investment yields $1,300 per year (as in comparison A), we assume that the returns gradually decline, as in Table 4-1. Again we vary $n$ from 4 to 20. When $n = 4$, the pretax income is $2,000 the first year, $1,900 the second year, $1,800 the third year and $1,700 the fourth year. When $n = 5$, the first four years return the above amounts and the fifth year returns $1,600.

TABLE 4-1

PRETAX RETURNS FROM A HYPOTHETICAL INVESTMENT

| Year | Return | Year | Return |
|------|--------|------|--------|
| 1    | $2,000 | 11   | $1,000 |
| 2    | 1,900  | 12   | 900    |
| 3    | 1,800  | 13   | 800    |
| 4    | 1,700  | 14   | 700    |
| 5    | 1,600  | 15   | 600    |
| 6    | 1,500  | 16   | 500    |
| 7    | 1,400  | 17   | 400    |
| 8    | 1,300  | 18   | 300    |
| 9    | 1,200  | 19   | 200    |
| 10   | 1,100  | 20   | 100    |

Again, an acquisition cost of $4,000, straight line depreciation, and a tax rate of 32 percent are assumed.

In the case of declining annual returns, a problem exists with respect to formulas assuming a constant $Q$ (posttax cash flow) in the face of the fact that $Q$ is declining. What is $Q$ when annual returns are not the same each year? We will use two different formulations of $Q$ in this case: (a) average annual posttax returns—for example if $n = 4$, then

$Q$ is $(Q_1 + Q_2 + Q_3 + Q_4) / 4$; (b) first year performance —this takes $Q_1$ as $Q$.

The payback reciprocal and rate of income on total investment are each computed using both average annual posttax returns and first year performance in the calculations.[18] Figure 4-3 shows the relationship between the discounted rate of return and the alternative methods. We consider each alternative separately.

1. *Payback reciprocal (average annual returns)*. There is an inverted relationship between the payback reciprocal and the discounted rate of return when the payback reciprocal is formulated with average annual returns used to compute $Q$. As the discounted rate of return rises, the payback reciprocal calculated on the basis of average returns falls. This is due to the fact that average annual returns (pretax and posttax) decline as $n$ increases. The accuracy of this measure is poor.

2. *Payback reciprocal (first year performance)*. Better estimates of the discounted rate of return result when first year performance is used to compute $Q$ in the payback reciprocal. For large $n$, the payback reciprocal using first year performance is within five percentage points of the discounted rate of return. For small $n$ the estimate is poor.

3. *Simple payback reciprocal*. For the case cited, the simple payback reciprocal is an excellent estimate of the discounted rate of return above an $n$ of nine years; there is only about a two or three percentage point difference between them. When $n$ is small, the difference becomes large and the estimate is poor.

---

[18] To illustrate how $Q_t$ was formulated when computing the discounted rate of return the following is included:

If $n = 4$, annual depreciation expense is $1,000. The postax cash flows $Q_t$ are

Year 1 = \$1,520   Year 3 = \$1,384   Year 5 = \$1,248   Year 7 = \$1,112
Year 2 = \$1,452   Year 4 = \$1,316   Year 6 = \$1,180   Year 8 = \$1,044

For each value of $n$ (usable life), annual depreciation expense changes and hence posttax returns for any given year also change.

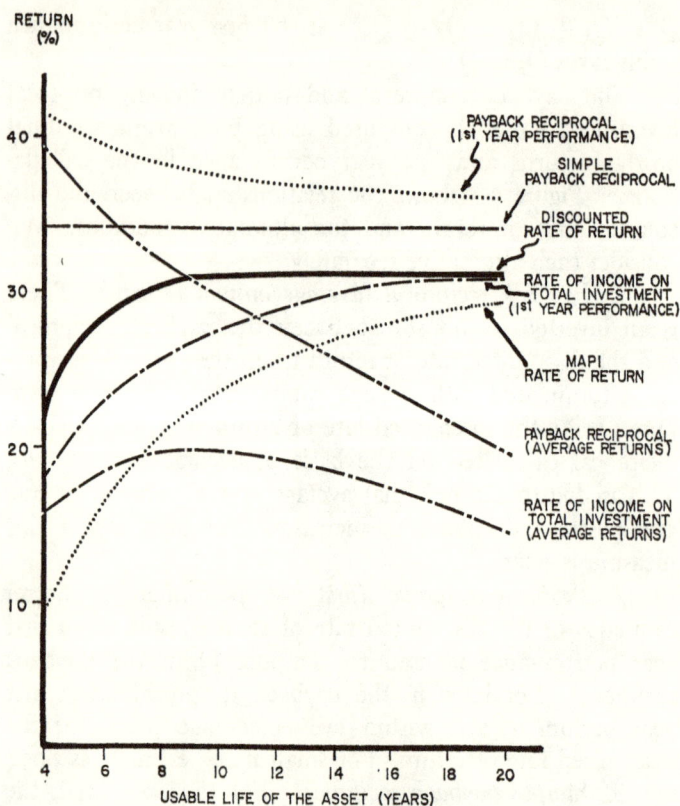

FIGURE 4-3

COMPARISON BETWEEN DISCOUNTED RATE OF RETURN AND
ALTERNATIVE METHODS—AN ASSET WITH DECLINING
ANNUAL PRETAX RETURNS

4. *The MAPI rate of return.* This is a good approximation to the discounted rate of return for most values of $n$ and
is best for very large $n$. The MAPI rate of return assumes a
decline in returns over the years, and thus is a better
approximation in comparison B than in comparison A. The
MAPI rate of return is unaffected by average returns since it
always uses first year performance.

5. *Rate of income on total investment (average annual*

*returns*). For most $n$, an inverted relationship appears with the discounted rate of return; in all cases where average returns are used to compute $Q$ (except very small $n$), rate of income on total investment is a poor estimate of the discounted rate of return. The relationship here is similar to the payback reciprocal that utilizes average annual returns.

6. *Rate of income on total investment (first year performance).* As shown in Figure 4-3, this is consistently the best estimate of the discounted rate of return under the assumptions of the comparison. When $n$ is large, it is almost identical. The divergence is at most six percentage points and generally is less than four percentage points.

7. *Rate of income on average investment* is not shown in Figure 4-3 for two reasons: (a) it is easily estimated by doubling the rate of income on total investment, (b) it is generally not an accurate estimate.

*Comparison C—accuracy of alternative measures relative to length of life of the investment—declining annual pretax returns with fixed depreciation period*

This case is similar to comparison B. Now, however, the depreciation expense is spread over a given number of years instead of the full life. Thus the annual accounting depreciation expense is no longer a declining function of length of life, but is fixed. Assume that the asset costs $4,000 and the tax rate is 32 percent. The asset is depreciated over four years when $n = 4$ and over five years when $n$ is between 5 and 20. The following relationships are found in Figure 4-4.

1. *The payback reciprocal (average annual returns)* has an inverted relationship with the discounted rate of return; any similarity between them is coincidental.

2. *The payback reciprocal (first year performance)* is constant at about 40 percent; it is not a close estimate of the discounted rate of return and is not shown in the figure.

3. *The simple payback reciprocal* is an amazingly close estimate of the discounted rate of return for an $n$ of more

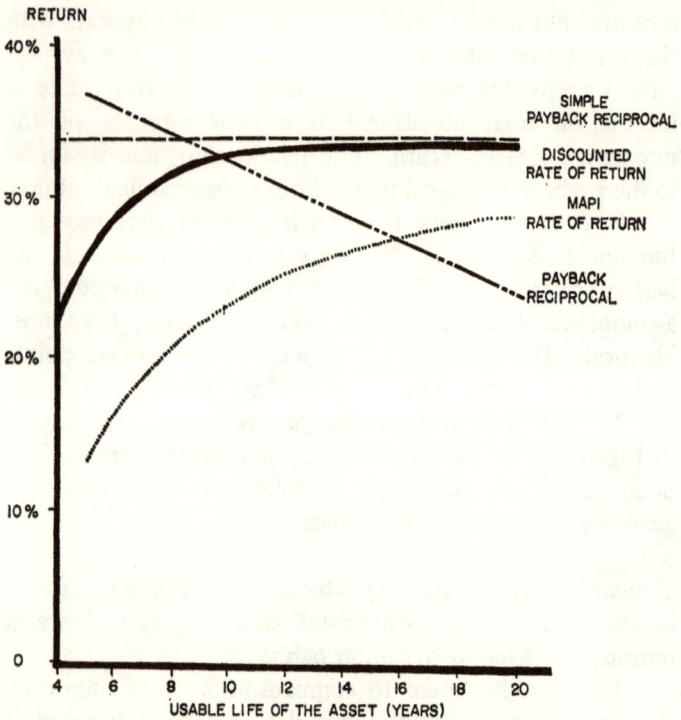

RETURN

40%

SIMPLE
PAYBACK RECIPROCAL

DISCOUNTED
RATE OF RETURN

MAPI
RATE OF RETURN

30%

PAYBACK
RECIPROCAL

20%

10%

0

4   6   8   10   12   14   16   18   20
USABLE LIFE OF THE ASSET (YEARS)

FIGURE 4-4

Comparison between Discounted Rate of Return and
Alternative Methods—an Asset with Declining
Annual Pretax Returns and Fixed
Depreciation Period

than eight or nine years. It is the best estimate in this case.

4. *The MAPI rate of return* provides a fairly good
estimate of the discounted rate of return (within five percentage points) when $n$ is large (20) and is closer for larger
$n$. There is a constant downward bias in the MAPI rate of
return of from five to eight percentage points.

5. *Rate of income on total investment (average annual
returns)* is not included in comparison C because there is no
one annual depreciation charge and hence no single computational procedure.

6. *Rate of income on total investment (first year performance)* is not a good estimate in comparison C. It is constant at about 20 percent and far from the discounted rate of return; it is also not shown in the figure.

*Summary of the three comparisons*

In all three of these comparisons, the simple payback reciprocal consistently provides an excellent estimate of the discounted rate of return for large $n$. It is ironic that the simplest formula should turn out to be one of the best estimators. The MAPI rate of return (in all three comparisons) and the rate of income on total investment utilizing first year performance (in the first two comparisons) provide fairly close estimates of the discounted rate of return; practical businessmen would probably not go wrong if they use these two alternative methods for estimating purposes. The payback reciprocal, if we use both average returns and first year performance in our calculations, does not compare favorably with the other alternative methods. Rate of income on average investment is a poor estimate of the discounted rate of return for large $n$ but a better estimate for small $n$.

*Twelve hypothetical investments: Comparisons of ranking*

Another approach to our evaluation of alternative methods is a comparison of their ranking ability. It is necessary that the reader be aware that we are drastically changing the direction of analysis. Previously we observed the accuracy of the alternative methods in estimating the discounted rate of return. Only one proposal was considered, and the only variable was the life of the project. Now a number of investment proposals are considered, each with a definite life and earnings stream. The alternative methods are now employed to rank these varied investment proposals, with present value as the standard of comparison. We identify these 12 projects by letter (A to L). We assume no terminal salvage value, straight line depreciation, and a 32

**TABLE 4-2**

**PRETAX RETURNS OF TWELVE INVESTMENTS**

| Project Cost Year | A $2,900 | B $4,500 | C $1,895 | D $2,800 | E $3,000 | F $3,000 | G $2,400 | H $2,000 | I $1,000 | J $950 | K $300 | L $450 |
|---|---|---|---|---|---|---|---|---|---|---|---|---|
| 1 | 1,000 | 1,600 | 500 | 1,000 | 400 | 800 | 800 | 800 | 300 | 300 | 100 | 200 |
| 2 | 1,000 | 1,400 | 500 | 900 | 400 | 750 | 800 | 700 | 300 | 290 | 100 | 190 |
| 3 | 1,000 | 1,200 | 500 | 800 | 400 | 700 | 800 | 600 | 300 | 280 | 100 | 180 |
| 4 | 1,000 | 1,000 | 500 | 700 | 400 | 650 | 800 | 500 | 300 | 270 | 100 | 170 |
| 5 | 1,000 | 800 | 500 | 600 | 400 | 600 | 800 | 400 | 300 | 260 | 100 | 160 |
| 6 | | | 500 | 500 | 400 | 550 | | | 300 | 250 | 100 | 150 |
| 7 | | | 500 | 400 | 400 | 500 | | | 300 | 240 | 100 | 140 |
| 8 | | | 500 | 300 | 400 | 450 | | | 300 | 230 | 100 | 130 |
| 9 | | | 500 | 200 | 400 | 400 | | | 300 | 220 | 100 | 120 |
| 10 | | | 500 | 100 | 400 | 350 | | | 300 | 210 | 100 | 110 |
| 11 | | | | | 400 | 300 | | | | | 100 | 100 |
| 12 | | | | | 400 | 250 | | | | | 100 | 90 |
| 13 | | | | | 400 | 200 | | | | | 100 | 80 |
| 14 | | | | | 400 | 150 | | | | | 100 | 70 |
| 15 | | | | | 400 | 100 | | | | | 100 | 60 |

percent tax rate. For tax purposes, proposals A, B, G, and H are depreciated over five years, C, D, I, and J over ten years, and E, F, K, and L over 15 years. In the computations, posttax returns (not shown) are used. Table 4-2 shows the pretax returns expected from each of 12 prospective proposals.

Table 4-3 shows the rankings, derived from computing values for formulas 1, 9, 10, 11, 12, 13, 14. Since both rate of income on average and total investment necessarily rank proposals alike, only the latter is used.

The projects (A to L) are ranked according to the assumed standard—the highest excess present value. The third column of Table 4-3 lists the discounted rates of return; there is only a slight divergence from the present value ranking. All alternative methods misrank these proposals, but this does not mean that all of them lead to serious error.

It is desirable to continue the analysis by separating the proposals into two groups: those with constant annual returns (A, C, E, G, I, and K) and those with declining annual returns (B, D, F, H, J, and L). The results of this division are shown in Table 4-4.

1. *Payback reciprocal* does not rank proposals in any systematic manner. All formulations of the payback reciprocal grossly misrank the proposals.

2. *The MAPI rate of return* misranks one investment in each category (proposals E and J). With these two exceptions, the MAPI rate of return ranks the proposals excellently.

3. *Rate of income on total investment (average annual returns)* correctly ranks proposals in the constant returns class. (There is no difference between first year performance and average annual returns when returns are constant.) One proposal (H) is misranked in the declining returns class.

4. *Rate of income on total investment (first year performance)* correctly ranks all of the proposals in the constant annual returns category and misranks one proposal with declining annual returns. It, too, seems to perform admirably

## TABLE 4-3
### RANKING OF TWELVE INVESTMENTS BY VARIOUS METHODS

| Rank | Excess present value as % of cost (discounted at 10%) | Discounted rate of return | Rate of income on total investment (First year performance) | Payback reciprocal | Rate of income on total investment (Average annual returns) | Payback reciprocal | Simple payback reciprocal | MAPI |
|------|------|------|------|------|------|------|------|------|
| 1 | K | L | L | H | K | A | L | L |
| 2 | L | K | K | L | L | G | H | K |
| 3 | I | I | D | B | I | H | D | D |
| 4 | J | J | J | A | J | K | B | F |
| 5 | C | C | I* | G | C | B | A | J |
| 6 | D | A | F* | D | A | I | K* | I |
| 7 | A | G | H* | K | G | L | I* | C |
| 8 | G | D | C | J | H | J | G* | H |
| 9 | F | F | B | I | D | C | J | B |
| 10 | H | H | A | C | F | D | F | A |
| 11 | B | B | G | F | B* | F | C | E |
| 12 | E | E | E | E | E* | E | E | G |

* Indicates investments with same rank.
For the actual values, see Appendix D.

when called upon to rank investment proposals. Since rate of income on average investment is found by doubling rate of income on total investment, these methods necessarily rank proposals in the same order.

5. *Discounted rate of return* correctly ranks all of the proposals when they are divided into the two groups. It does not always perform so well; if one desires, he can contrive a situation in which every proposal is misranked by the discounted rate of return, but in an actual situation such misranking is unlikely.

Perhaps the most serious drawback of the alternative methods is that they do not tell us exactly when proposals are absolutely unprofitable (such as proposals B and E). Complete reliance on alternative methods may be misleading since they do not indicate the cutoff point of profitability. The answer to this problem lies in having available many highly profitable alternative proposals so that the best are surely profitable.

Perhaps small businessmen generally deal with proposals whose returns are either constant or declining; if so, alternative methods may rank satisfactorily in practical cases. These 12 proposals were not selected to produce a particular result; there was no juggling to find proposals that rank poorly or rank well. Thus considerable justification for the use of some alternative methods in small firms seems to exist; a later chapter presents additional evidence in favor of these alternative formulas.

The present value standard used here has several limitations itself. It is based on an arbitrary discounting rate of 10 percent. If other rates are used, different rankings result. There is always uncertainty about the appropriate discounting rate, which is not only a measure of present opportunity cost, but is also the future rate at which returns from these proposals can be invested. A slight mistake in prediction of future opportunity cost changes the ranking of these proposals. In addition, the present value method is based on simplifying assumptions that do

TABLE 44

**RANKING OF TWELVE INVESTMENTS BY VARIOUS METHODS, GROUPED ACCORDING TO CONSTANT ANNUAL RETURNS AND DECLINING ANNUAL RETURNS**

| Rank | Excess present value as % of % of discounted cost (discounted at 10%) | Discounted rate of return | Rate of income on total investment (First year performance) | Payback reciprocal | Rate of income on total investment (Average annual returns) | Payback reciprocal | Simple payback reciprocal | MAPI |
|---|---|---|---|---|---|---|---|---|
| | | | CONSTANT ANNUAL RETURNS | | | | | |
| 1 | K | K | K | A | K | A | A | K |
| 2 | I | I | I | G | I | G | K* | I |
| 3 | C | C | C | K | C | K | I* | C |
| 4 | A | A | A | I | A | I | G* | A |
| 5 | G | G | G | C | G | C | C | G |
| 6 | E | E | E | E | E | E | E | E |
| | | | DECLINING ANNUAL RETURNS | | | | | |
| 1 | L | L | L | H | L | H | L | L |
| 2 | J | J | D | L | J | B | H | D |
| 3 | D | D | J | B | H | L | D | F |
| 4 | F | F | F* | D | D | J | B | J |
| 5 | H | H | H* | J | F | D | J | H |
| 6 | B | B | B | F | B | F | F | B |

* Indicates investments with same rank.
For the actual values, see Appendix D.

not fit practical cases; therefore, the standard of accuracy leaves much to be desired, although it is the best criterion available. Thus, there is no panacea in investment decisions. All analyses require judgment, even when using methods of ranking investment proposals that are theoretically correct.

*Summary and conclusion*

The cost of the information necessary, the training required, and the time involved probably make the use of refined formulas uneconomical for the small businessman. With this in mind, we believe that a cheaper (and perhaps less accurate) formula is almost a necessity. It has been shown in this chapter that—(for the cases illustrated) when the length of life is relatively long—the best estimates of the discounted rate of return are the simple payback reciprocal, rate of income on total investment (using first year performance), and the MAPI rate of return; rate of income on average investment is a better estimate when length of life is relatively short.

We have seen that the simple payback reciprocal is an excellent estimate of the discounted rate of return when the length of life is long but that it ranks proposals poorly.

When we rank a group of investments, some of which are short lived and others long lived, the payback reciprocal is quite unreliable. We do not recommend any of the three forms of the payback reciprocal illustrated as a measure of relative profitability when both short- and long-lived proposals are to be ranked[19] *and* when future costs and revenues can be reasonably estimated.

[19] In this respect, we feel that Gordon has unintentionally oversold the payback reciprocal to some of his colleagues. He has shown that its estimating power is sometimes excellent. Under conditions of certainty, the truly important test is its ranking power. It seems that the payback reciprocal is incapable of satisfactory ranking when lives of proposals differ. Some of the other alternative methods rank well but estimate poorly, for example, rate of income on average investment. A proposal is not really profitable unless it is both absolutely and relatively profitable. Later we attempt to justify the payback period as a rationing measure, but for different reasons.

The MAPI rate of return[20] and rate of income on total and average investment seem to rank investments adequately when they are divided into the two groups because, as shown in Figures 4-2, 4-3, and 4-4, the curvature of these functions follows the same pattern as the discounted rate of return. Although they are sometimes poor estimates, their ranking ability is not impaired by this lack of accuracy. Even before the constant and declining returns dichotomy, rate of income on total investment ranked proposals fairly well. We have not shown here that alternative methods are better than theoretically correct formulations; our purpose has been to raise doubt about the traditional viewpoint that alternative methods are too crude and inaccurate to be useful.[21]

Much may be said, in conclusion, for substituting the rate of income on investment or the MAPI rate of return for the discounted rate of return or present value methods, especially in the case of small business. Here we have considered only the case of certainty in a proposal's returns. Uncertainty further complicates the problem of ranking and provides further justification for the use of simpler methods. The evaluation of actual business practice will thus not always rest on the most refined methods and concepts, but more often on those approaches that provide reasonably effective results.

[20] Although the MAPI rate of return is conceptually difficult, it is computationally easy.

[21] Bierman and Smidt, 13-32, examine the ranking ability of a few alternative methods. Even though some methods rank proposals well in their analysis, the authors quickly dismiss them. The authors are, we think, too anxious to "sell" the present value method. While they frankly admit that present value has serious limitations, they overlook the importance and applicability of alternative methods in business practice.

*5*

## SOME EMPIRICAL STUDIES OF
## INVESTMENT DECISIONS

*A*LTHOUGH none of the empirical studies of investment decisions are concerned with small business, a review of the practices of large firms will be helpful in establishing a framework of reference and a point of departure for the empirical consideration of small business. Many economic principles hold true regardless of the size of the firm, yet it is also true that the small firm is not simply a miniature version of the large one and the economies of its operation must necessarily differ. The studies of big business have been of three types: surveys of rationing methods, case studies of investment decisions, and research on the determinants of investment, the last of which is not pertinent to our present investigation.

## SURVEYS OF RATIONING METHODS

*In the* surveys of rationing methods it is interesting that large firms rely heavily on the payback approach; few use such refined techniques as the discounted rate of return or present value. The two surveys discussed here are not random samples but do give some insight into the methods used by big business.

*MAPI surveys*

The Machinery and Allied Products Institute conducted questionnaire surveys of business practice in replacement and depreciation in 1948 and 1956.[1] Information from over 200 large firms comprised the survey data. The percentage of firms responding yes to some of the questions are tabulated below.

| Methods | 1948 | 1956 |
|---|---|---|
| Payback | 42 | 60 |
| Minimum-average-cost | 8 | 24 |
| MAPI | 19 | 47 |
| Discounted rate of return | 1 | 2 |

| Other | | |
|---|---|---|
| Is there an individual with special responsibility for equipment studies in your firm? | 28 | 54 |
| Do you perform annual equipment reviews? | 35 | 79 |

The authors state that there is a trend toward more "dynamic" equipment policies, because more firms used

[1] *Equipment Replacement and Depreciation—A Survey of Policies and Practices* (Washington, D. C.: Machinery and Allied Products Institute and Council for Technological Advancement, 1956).

analytical techniques in 1956 than in 1948. Both surveys showed a large number of firms using the payback formula.

*Miller survey*

The Miller survey deals with methods used by 127 "well-managed" companies.[2] Although it considers many types of decisions, we shall concentrate on that portion related to capital investments. Miller made use of ten different rationing methods, listed below with the number of companies employing each:

| Method | No. using |
|---|---|
| Payback | 66 |
| Discounted cash flow | 38 |
| Return on total assets at original cost | 59 |
| Return on total assets at book value | 0 |
| Return on total assets at estimated replacement cost | 0 |
| Return on total assets at original cost less current liability | 15 |
| Return on total assets at book value less current liability | 0 |
| Return on total assets at replacement cost less current liability | 1 |
| Return on net worth | 2 |
| Other methods | 6 |

Of the 127 companies, 63 use only one method, 36 use two methods, 16 use three, and one uses more than three.

*Critique of the surveys*

Both of these surveys have limited significance since the questionnaire method is itself a limitation and is not suited to revealing the actualities of decision making. Persons responding to the questionnaire may not understand the questions, and, more importantly, many questions cannot be

[2] James H. Miller, "A Glimpse at Practice in Calculating and Using Return on Investment," *N.A.A. Bulletin*, XLII (June 1960), 20.

answered by a yes or no or by a check mark. Also, few company officials want to admit that their policy or practice is deficient. In defense, they may give an "academic" answer even though it is not a correct description of their practice. Furthermore, it is perhaps significant that each of these two surveys finds a different "mix" of methods. It is not surprising that only the MAPI survey finds application of the MAPI system; its questionnaires were sent to capital goods manufacturers more familiar with the MAPI approach. Nor is it surprising that an accountant like Miller should find widespread use of methods publicized in the accounting literature. Finally, neither of the surveys attempts to indicate how the firms actually made use of the various rationing techniques.

These surveys can hardly be called a representative sample of business practice; the answers to questions were probably solicited from firms with better than average management. The surveys do, however, give some picture of the methods used by big business. They seem to indicate that much attention is being given to investment decisions even though the uses of payback period and other relatively crude methods of rationing prevail.

## CASE STUDIES OF INVESTMENT
## DECISION MAKING

We now turn our attention to four case studies that delve with varying degrees of thoroughness into investment decisions. By limiting this section to four studies, much interesting material is omitted. Dozens of case studies of individual firms are listed by the Intercollegiate Case Clearing House at Harvard University; to date no one has analyzed them for the purpose of summarizing actual company practices. Many other interview and statistical studies have been published, but most are concerned with determinants of investment. Still other studies relate to the financing of business investment and other topics that are given only passing attention in this volume.

*N.A.A. study*

The National Association of Accountants study covers 44 large companies and includes a textbook discussion of rate of income formulas and of the discounted rate of return.[3] Of the 44 firms, 42 use rate of income formulations for analyzing past investments. Some of the firms use the discounted rate of return with a high degree of refinement; the exact number is not revealed.

The most significant finding in the study is that although most of the firms use rationing methods that might be considered crude, they do so in a rather sophisticated way. Several interviews, reproduced in the N.A.A. report, indicate that substantial thought and resources have been allocated to the rationing process. Some company officials recognize the relationship between the payback period and the discounted rate of return. For example, one executive stated that a four-year payback is, under certain conditions, essentially a 25 percent discounted rate of return. Other officials adjust the payback criterion according to the life of the proposal. The fact that most firms do not use refined methods may indicate that their managements do not believe a high degree of refinement would be beneficial.

*A study of four investment decisions*

Cyert, Dill, and March describe four investment decisions of three different large firms.[4] The information was gathered through analysis of written company matter, intensive personal interviews, and direct observation. The four decisions concern equipment replacement, new quarters for a department, selection of a consulting firm, and choice of data processing equipment. Several conclusions are drawn from the vast amount of data on these four decisions.

[3] National Association of Accountants, *Return on Capital as a Guide to Managerial Decisions*, N.A.A. Research Report No. 35, December 1959.

[4] R. M. Cyert, W. R. Dill, and J. G. March, "The Role of Expectations in Business Decision Making," *Administrative Science Quarterly*, III (December 1958), 307-40.

1. Refined capital rationing techniques were not employed; had they been used, the decisions probably would not have been much different.

2. Two investments arose through crisis and the other two through planning. In all four decisions considerable time and effort were expended on search activity.

3. Consequences of particular acts were computed quite simply; i.e., elaborate analysis was not employed. The comparison of relative advantage was difficult because of the different dimensions of the benefits. Therefore, quantification of these benefits was likely to prove fruitless.

4. There was usually a comparison of the proposal with a few other alternatives. We shall see later that small firms do not seem to weigh simultaneously the advantages and disadvantages of various alternative investments.

*Large firms in the Twin Cities area*

Walter W. Heller conducted interviews with key decision makers of large firms with headquarters in the Twin Cities area.[5] He notes increased emphasis on systematic capital budgeting procedures. Heller distinguishes between the physical budget (demand for funds) and financial budget (supply of funds). About half of the companies used a physical budget and a "formal-but-flexible" financial budget. Heller concludes that three factors lead to adoption of capital budgeting techniques: the size of the firm, tight working capital position, and the degree of separation of ownership and management. Approval of projects, he finds, depends upon the amount of the expenditure, and past mistakes are instrumental in policy decisions. Some firms decentralized screening of investments because management was cluttering itself with so many minor projects that it could not take a broad perspective. Other firms centralized screening because of mistakes and "empire building" by subordinates.

[5] Walter W. Heller, "The Anatomy of Investment Decisions," *Harvard Business Review*, XXX (March 1951), 95-103.

Most firms that Heller investigated used the payback approach, but some felt that any formula was unwise; instead they relied exclusively upon judgment. Where protection of working capital was important, the firms favored the projects with the shortest payback periods.

Two factors seem to relate most directly to small business: size and separation of ownership and management. Heller believes that as these two factors increase, systematic capital budgeting becomes more important. If this relationship prevails, it helps explain why small firms do not make more use of rationing systems.

### A study of 48 large firms

Personal interviews with 147 officials in 48 extremely large corporations, chosen from the *Fortune* "Directory" of July 1957, comprised the basis for a study by Istvan.[6]

Only nine firms used a long range capital budget; Istvan interprets this to mean that the firms are shortsighted—they are too much concerned with the immediate future. A more likely explanation is that long range predictions are so vague or difficult as to be of little value.

Five of the firms used the discounted rate of return. Nine others indicated they use it only for large expansion projects. Only two firms used the MAPI rate of return, 32 used rate of income on total investment, and 34 used the payback period. One executive who used the discounted rate of return stated that the chief difficulty lay in determining the advantages of an investment proposal; after determining them, he found one method about as complicated as another.

Two observations are particularly interesting and closely related to small business. All 48 firms indicated that most investment proposals come from operating personnel and not top management. Only one firm exerted special effort to

[6] Donald Frank Istvan, "The Capital-Expenditure Decision-Making Process in Forty-Eight Large Corporations" (unpublished Ph.D. dissertation, School of Business, Indiana University, 1959).

55

insure a backlog of investment proposals. In the other firms there was always a backlog of desirable investments awaiting implementation.

The small firm has few employees who can submit proposals; perhaps this is a major reason it does not possess a backlog of possible investments.

## CONCLUSION

*The experience* of large firms raises several points of interest in evaluating small business practice.

1. Most large firms do not use refined capital rationing techniques. Instead, shortcut methods such as payback period, MAPI rate of return, or rate of income on investment are substituted.

2. There may be a relationship between systematic capital budgeting and factors such as size and degree of separation of ownership and management.

3. Because a continual flow of proposals comes in from members of the entire organization, large firms probably do not devote much top level time and effort to searching for profitable investment opportunities.

4. When an investment proposal is analyzed in a large company, a great amount of time is often spent, although the analysis may not be highly systematic.

In many areas of capital budgeting, the small firm is handicapped by the lack of specialization. If large firms cannot or do not apply economic theory in a careful way, we can hardly expect that the small company, limited in personnel and facilities, will be able to do so.

# 6

## UNCERTAINTY AND ERRORS
## OF ESTIMATION

$W$E HAVE shown earlier that the simpler techniques for investment evaluation may be useful tools of analysis; some provide relatively close estimates of the discounted rate of return and rank proposals in nearly the same order as would present value analysis. Even though these simpler, alternative methods are close approximations to refined measures, they are still approximations. Initially we answered this argument by indicating that the extra time and training necessary to use refined analysis cannot generally be afforded by the small businessman. Now we argue that the theoretical methods have limited practical value *because of the uncertainty involved in making the estimates* required for the analysis.

There is general agreement that if estimates of investment parameters such as costs, revenues, length of life, salvage value, and cost of capital can be made accurately, theoretical methods of investment analysis are advantageous. First, let us assume that the trained manpower and computer facilities are available to perform the refined analysis recommended by most of the capital budgeting literature. Then the big question is: *with the degree of uncertainty that appears in most estimated figures, how useful are the concepts of discounted rate of return and present value?* Obviously, the answer requires that we estimate the uncertainty involved. We do this in four steps:

(a) determination of the degree of uncertainty in some of the small business cases;

(b) an attempt to determine the effect of errors of estimation on the discounted rate of return or present value;

(c) a review of four possible approaches to the subject of decision making under uncertainty in an attempt to find better methods of analysis in investment decisions; and,

(d) a rationale of the payback period in terms of uncertainty.

## CASES ILLUSTRATING DEGREES OF UNCERTAINTY IN INVESTMENT PARAMETERS

*This* section deals with five case studies, each of which involves uncertainty. Cases 1 and 2 are situations in which annual returns and life are uncertain, but estimates of them were quantified by the interviewees. In these we seek to determine how much error in estimates it is reasonable to assume. Case 3 is concerned with uncertainty, but here the interviewee did not quantify his estimates. Case 4 involves relatively little uncertainty, thus providing some balance. Case 5 is presented to show how, in one firm, the problem of estimation is circumvented. For purposes of simplification we concern ourselves with uncertainty in only two investment parameters: annual pretax returns and the length of time that these returns continue (or more simply, length of life).[1]

## Case 1, a coin-operated laundry

Mr. X was presented with a proposal to open a coin-operated, self-service laundry consisting of 50 washers and 20 dryers. A desirable location was available at the time. Costs were fairly certain. The total investment was to be about $40,000, of which $5,000 was for installation cost and the remainder for washers, dryers, and other equipment. Expenses were $900 per month rent, $300 per month for utilities (depending upon use), and miscellaneous expenses of about $200 per month. The cash investment was $15,000, and the other $25,000 was to be financed at 6 percent interest over a three-year period; the annual principal and interest payment would amount to about $9,400. Demand was the most uncertain variable. A survey by Mr. X of other coin-operated laundries in the surrounding area revealed that with 20 washers the average revenue was about $1,500 per month and that with 50 washers the monthly revenue ranged from $3,000 to $6,000. Mr. X estimated that at the very worst his monthly revenue would be $2,500, but since he had a choice location, $3,000 to $3,500 was his best estimate of monthly revenue.

We gather Mr. X's figures together under four columns according to demand $(D_1, D_2, D_3, D_4)$.

|  | $D_1$ | $D_2$ | $D_3$ | $D_4$ |
|---|---|---|---|---|
| Annual sales revenue | $30,000 | $40,000 | $48,000 | $60,000 |
| Principal and interest | $ 9,400 | $ 9,400 | $ 9,400 | $ 9,400 |
| Rent | 10,800 | 10,800 | 10,800 | 10,800 |
| Utilities and misc. | 6,000 | 9,000 | 10,000 | 14,000 |
| Total cost | $26,200 | $29,200 | $30,200 | $34,200 |
| Profit estimates* | $ 3,800 | $ 8,800 | $17,800 | $25,800 |

* The figures shown are not really net profits. Principal payments are deducted from revenue. This was Mr. X's method of analysis which was more concerned with cash flow than with net profits.

[1] Engineering economists maintain that economic life is the solution to an equation. Implied in this assertion, however, is an accurate prediction of costs and revenues. Furthermore, if technology terminates cash flow, the mathematical treatment of economic life may be inapplicable.

Another uncertain aspect of this case is the length of life of the washers and dryers. Searching for this information, Mr. X found that the life of coin laundry equipment seemed to range from two to six years and that generally these washers and dryers had no salvage value when discarded.

*Theoretical analysis.* First let us compute the discounted rate of return for the first case illustration.[2] The problem is that we have many possible situations to contend with, depending on the revenue and life estimate. The discounted rate of return for each of the 20 situations[3] is shown in Table 6-1.

After all of these computations (which incidentally would take hours to perform without an electronic computer), how much closer are we to a solution? Table 6-1 tells us that if annual revenue does not exceed $30,000, the proposal may be unprofitable; it may even be unprofitable if revenue is $40,000. If annual revenue exceeds $48,000 and cost estimates prove correct, the venture will be profitable, even if the machines last only two years.

[2] In order to compute the discounted rate of return accurately, the reinvestment rate (about 5 percent) must be explicitly considered. The discounted rate of return assumes that the resulting rate of return is also the reinvestment rate. Consequently, some error creeps into the computations, but does not affect our conclusions.

[3] Mr. X was interested only in the return of his $15,000 cash investment rather than his total investment of $40,000. We compute the discounted rate of return for each of these 20 situations using the entire investment of $40,000 as a base. We also use different profit figures from Mr. X's, eliminating the deduction for principal. Pretax profits (before depreciation) are shown below.

| Year | $D_1$ | $D_2$ | $D_3$ | $D_4$ |
|------|-------|-------|-------|-------|
| 1 | $11,700 | $19,700 | $25,700 | $33,700 |
| 2 | 12,174 | 20,174 | 26,174 | 34,174 |
| 3 | 12,686 | 20,676 | 26,676 | 34,676 |
| 4 | 13,200 | 21,200 | 27,200 | 35,200 |
| 5 | 13,200 | 21,200 | 27,200 | 35,200 |
| 6 | 13,200 | 21,200 | 27,200 | 35,200 |

The assumptions are an investment of $40,000, a tax rate of 32 percent, and straight line depreciation. Posttax cash flows, used in the discounted rate of return computations, are computed from the formula $(R_t - D)(1 - T) + D + i$ as outlined in Chapter 4.

## TABLE 6-1
### Discounted Rates of Return, Coin-operated Laundry Case

| Annual receipts or revenue | $30,000 | $40,000 | $48,000 | $60,000 |
|---|---|---|---|---|
| Length of life: | | | | |
| 2 years | Negative | Negative | .132 | .302 |
| 3 " | Negative | .166 | .300 | .470 |
| 4 " | .064 | .253 | .382 | .546 |
| 5 " | .119 | .300 | .424 | .581 |
| 6 " | .154 | .328 | .447 | .598 |

*Practical analysis.* Mr. X did not need Table 6-1. He came to a similar conclusion, without such precise analysis, by using the payback period. His main concern was the length of time required for his cash investment ($15,000) to be returned. He reasoned that if annual receipts (sales) were $35,000, his investment would be returned in two years. If annual receipts were $45,000, his investment would be returned in one year. "After the cash investment is returned, all returns are gravy." His judgment told him that adequate sales levels would probably be reached, making the investment profitable.[4]

The important point here is that an error equal to 5 or 10 percent of the original investment in Mr. X's best estimate of profits could turn a seemingly profitable proposal into a marginal or unprofitable one.[5] Mr. X felt confident that

[4] Other considerations were important here also. This investment required little supervisory time, something that Mr. X could not spare. The cash outlay ($15,000) was as large as Mr. X was willing to spend. Other proposals were considered, but they required either more cash or more supervisory time.

[5] Note 2 above shows the actual pretax profits (before depreciation). A 5-10 percent estimating error in pretax returns would not seem unlikely. For example, at $40,000 sales volume ($D_2$), pretax profits (before depreciation) for the first year would be $19,700; for $30,000 ($D_1$), first year pretax profits would be $11,700. This is an $8,000 difference. Using $40,000 (the amount of investment) as a base, the error would be more than 20 percent. No matter how the error is determined, it would be sizable.

annual receipts of $30,000 were extremely unlikely and that receipts of $60,000 were equally improbable. He considered $36,000 to $40,000 the most likely revenue estimate, and he knew that if this were the case, the investment would be quite lucrative.

There was not enough money at stake to warrant a reliable market research study; perhaps if any estimates were to be made, Mr. X could forecast as accurately as anyone else. He had studied the market, the consumer's habits, operation of the business, and costs of operation through personal contacts with other owners, consumers, and factory representatives. Even with all of this information at his disposal, his estimates were conjectural and a sizable error was quite possible. A 5 or 10 percent error in annual pretax profits (as a percentage of original investment) and a two- to three-year error in length of life would seem to be well within the scope of probable errors in this case.

The argument up to this point has been that with the amount of uncertainty present in Mr. X's estimates, a high degree of quantitative refinement would be both unnecessary and inaccurate. The payback period seemed to perform essentially the same function as refined analysis. This case provides an actual instance in which the use of refined techniques would have been a waste of time and effort.

It seems clear that the dominant role of personal judgment, the factor that theoretical measures attempt to eliminate through quantification, will continue to override any mathematical calculations when uncertainty obscures the accuracy of investment parameters. Some cases are amenable to these methods if they are not obviously very profitable or unprofitable, but such situations appear to be exceptions.

*More detailed analysis.* The reader may wish a more detailed analysis to support the conclusion that in uncertain situations such as Case 1, refined analysis has little to contribute to investment decisions.

Mr. X stated that his best estimate of receipts (sales)

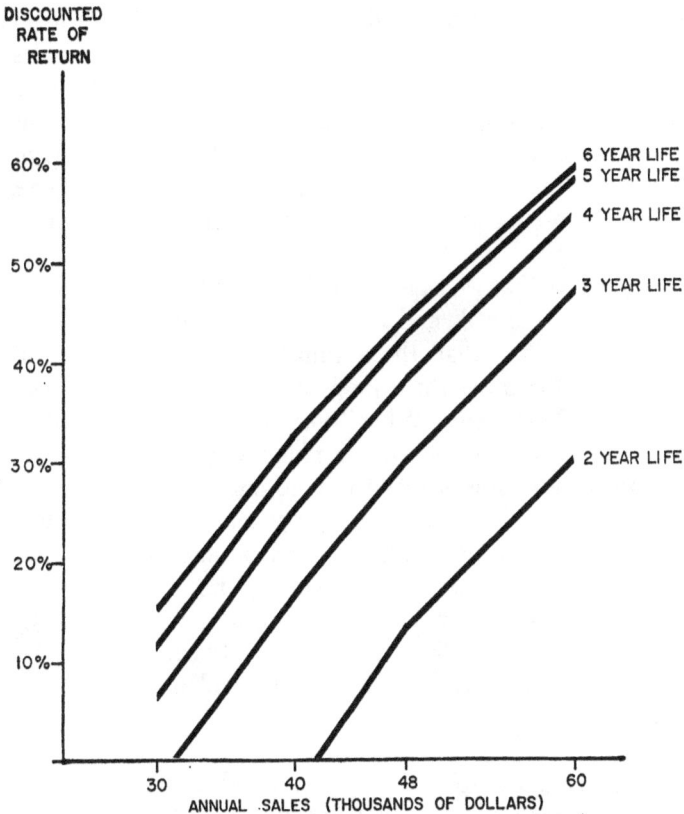

FIGURE 6-1

The Effect of Estimating Errors on the
Discounted Rate of Return—Case 1

was between $36,000 and $40,000 and life estimates ranged
from two to six years. If we examine Figure 6-1, which plots
data from Table 6-1, we find that within this range the
discounted rate of return varies from a negative figure to
about 33 percent.[6] This means that there is more than a 33

[6] If one is interested in the variation produced in the present value,
the excess present value as a percentage of cost varies from a negative
figure to 105 percent between $36,000 and $40,000 sales.

percentage point range in the discounted rate of return *on the same investment proposal*, within the indicated sales volumes. Even if we restrict the life to between three and five years, the range of the discounted rates of return is about 21 percentage points.[7] If this much variability is present in the evaluation of one investment proposal, how can we expect theoretical measures to add significant precision to our ranking?

Suppose that we have available four different prospective investment proposals and the coin laundry is among them. Suppose further that the estimated discounted rates of return for the other three proposals are 14 percent, 21 percent, and 26 percent. Where does the laundry proposal fit into the ranking? The answer requires personal judgment. Imagine the confusion if all four of our proposals have the same amount of variability in rate of return that was found in Case 1. Objective ranking would be impossible because no significant difference exists among the rates of return. Thus it seems unreasonable to ask the small businessman to rank proposals according to refined quantitative criteria. He does rank proposals, but in a simpler and more subjective manner.

*Case 2, a branch store*

This case presents uncertainty similar to that of the first case illustration.

A small businessman was thinking about opening a branch store in a new shopping center. He could estimate most of his major costs and the investment necessary. He hesitated, however, because demand was uncertain. To him, market research appeared too costly. He looked at the prospective location, talked to several associates, and computed a break-even point. He estimated monthly expenses as follows: rent $200, advertising $35, labor $190, utilities $70, and cost of goods 58 percent of sales. He felt that the worst sales outcome would be $500 per

[7] When the life is restricted to between three and five years, the range in excess present value as a percentage of cost is about 30 percentage points between $36,000 and $40,000 sales.

week and the best could possibly be $2,000 per week. Most likely sales ranged between $700 and $1,500 per week. He estimated fixed costs at about $120 per week. He reasoned that if sales reached $285, he would break even. At only $500 per week sales, an annual profit of $4,600 would result. The total investment required would be only $3,000. With such a short payback period, the proposal was accepted.[8] He assumed that the store would last a minimum of four to five years and possibly as long as 20 years.

Although this proposal is apparently quite profitable, great variability is possible in profits. If weekly sales are $700, $1,000, or $1,500, annual pretax profits amount to about $9,000, $16,000, or $27,000 respectively. As in Case 1, any theoretically correct measure for ranking this proposal against others conveys very little meaning. A 100 percent error (as a percentage of cost) in annual profits would appear to be a conservative estimate of probable error in this case; even greater error in length of life is reasonable.

### Case 3, a branch store

The next case illustrates a somewhat different type of uncertainty: uncertainty when estimates cannot easily be quantified.

Mr. Y, a variety store operator, owned three stores in a large city. A real estate agent came to him with a proposition concerning an available store in a relatively small town about 30 miles from his office. Mr. Y visited the small town one afternoon; he examined the merchandising procedures and relative location of the other stores in the area. He decided that the existing promotional techniques were outmoded and unaggressive. Merchandising management seemed inadequate. He reasoned that enough business could be taken from these other stores to make a store of his own very profitable. Mr. Y recognized the fact that retaliation would occur, but said that once he was entrenched, he could not be stopped. The rental was quite reasonable, and Mr. Y, with many years of experience, decided to invest. The investment was sizable; it consisted of

[8] Here other considerations were important. The proposal was in his line of business. He seemed nervous about capital investments in other industries. He did invest occasionally in listed securities.

fixtures, merchandise, and working capital. On the other hand, if necessary, the merchandise could be liquidated through his other stores and the fixtures used elsewhere. He believed that the maximum possible loss was unlikely and that sizable profits were probable.

On the basis of past experience, Mr. Y concluded that even simple quantitative analysis was unnecessary. He was quite confident that the necessary sales could be manipulated through proper merchandise management. The chance of failure was so small compared with the expected chances of success that Mr. Y had little trouble in making the decision. Since he had expanded in this manner before, the experience was not new. Many of the uncertainties involved had probably been dispelled by Mr. Y in some previous expansion. This decision was based on personal judgment, and again it was probably a sound investment.[9] Yet even Mr. Y would have to concede that a sizable error in estimates of returns and length of life was possible and therefore refined quantitative analysis would be of little help here.

*Case 4, a new machine*

This case involved little uncertainty. It is included to balance the perspective and give an example of a decision based on costs rather than demand.

The QRS Company is a fairly large manufacturer of wearing apparel. Mr. S, manager of the engineering department, makes all equipment investment decisions. Early in 1959, the QRS Company was buying about 100,000 labels per year for their garments at a cost of 1.5 cents per label. A new machine was presented by a salesman who estimated that it could produce 10,000 labels per day for about 0.5 cents each. The machine cost $3,000. Within a few days, Mr. S had lined up enough

[9] Nonmonetary considerations are extremely important here. Mr. Y is in his later years. He has no children. He mentioned the fact that a larger store in a larger town might be more profitable, but at his stage of life with no children, he felt no need for creating a tough competitive struggle in a larger town. He also believed that he could benefit the citizens in this small town by bringing them a fresh type of marketing and forcing his competitors to do the same.

label orders from other firms to pay for the machine in about six months and decided to purchase the machine.

The uncertainty found here is probably so slight that anything more than a few quick "back-of-the-envelope" calculations would seem unnecessary. The proposal is obviously very profitable, and although refined calculations may be possible (even though length of life would be difficult to predict), they would not be any more useful than the methods that were used.

*Similarities and dissimilarities: a summary*

In the laundry and branch store cases a 20 percent error in pretax returns (as a percentage of investment) would not be surprising. Since variation in costs was not considered, the errors in the discounted rates of return are probably greater. Useful length of life estimates may be even more difficult to assess than returns; the errors in life in these three cases could easily range from two to three years. Case 4 contained much less uncertainty.

The decision makers paid little attention to the length of life of the proposals in all four cases. While the payback period was used in the laundry and the first branch store cases, definite estimates of life were not really important in the decisions. In each of the four cases, the decision was unaffected by whether the estimated returns would continue for three years or ten years. No predictions far into the future were required or attempted for any of these proposals. This point is not unique; few proposals, throughout our interviews, involved prediction for more than two years unless there was an assurance of large terminal salvage values.

*Case 5, a further discussion of length of life and the payback period*

Other cases point out more explicitly the unwillingness of management to forecast the future when uncertainty is involved. This is exemplified by the following case.

The Z Company is a relatively large manufacturer of food products. It is departmentalized and employs about 150 people. Mr. Z, president of the firm, outlined his policy on investment decisions in terms of the pretax payback period.

Investment proposals are classified into three main groups. Class I projects cost $100 or less and are expected to pay for themselves in one year or less. Class II projects cost more than $100 but are expected to pay for themselves in one year or less. Class III projects include all others. Class I projects are automatically accepted, Class II projects are usually accepted, and Class III proposals are usually *not* accepted. Class II and III projects require written justification; Class I projects do not. The person submitting each proposal is required to prepare a written justification and is held responsible for the accuracy of any predictions made therein. Annually there is a postaudit of previously accepted projects. The interviewer looked at several proposals that had been accepted and found no inconsistencies between company policy and practice.

Thus, company policy discourages longrun forecasts and precludes consideration of returns far into the future. This means some proposals that might be profitable (because of their long life) are rejected. Because an official of the company is held responsible for the accuracy of estimates, it would seem that the company seldom risks its capital in extremely uncertain investments.

These firms seemingly give low priority to large, uncertain, future returns and high priority to small, more certain returns; employment of the payback period tends to confirm this viewpoint. Probably few small businessmen know of any other rationing method; at least, none who were interviewed used other rationing measures. Although the payback period has been severely criticized as theoretically unsound, its use under conditions of uncertainty may have sound justification.

## A MORE GENERAL ANALYSIS OF ESTIMATING ERRORS

*Up to this* point we have concerned ourselves with particular cases. We now attempt to establish more generally that errors in returns and length of life sharply reduce the usefulness of refined methods of rationing capital. Two types of investments are considered: investments with constant annual returns and investments with declining annual returns. The discussion centers on two hypothetical illustrations, covering a period of 20 years, purposely framed so that we can calculate the percentage error in returns. We continue to ignore errors in salvage values; while they are often significant, errors in life and returns are probably more important to the small businessman.

*Proposals with constant annual returns*

Suppose we estimate that an investment proposal will yield $1,000 annual pretax returns[10] for seven years. Assuming a cost of $4,000, a 32 percent tax rate, straight line depreciation, and no terminal salvage value, the posttax discounted rate of return is 11.6 percent. Now if the returns continue for only six years, all else remaining equal, the actual discounted rate of return is only 9.1 percent. This means that the actual return is 2.5 percentage points less than the estimate. Suppose that the returns continue for the predicted seven years but the investment returns $800 per year (before taxes) instead of the estimated $1,000; in this case the actual posttax discounted rate of return is 6.5 percent or 5.1 percentage points less than our original estimate of 11.6 percent.[11] There is a plethora of possible combinations of returns, lengths of life, and rates of return. The simplest way to illustrate these relationships is to graph them as in Figure 6-2. Along the vertical axis is the discounted rate of return, and along the horizontal axis is the error in the estimate of annual pretax returns as a percentage of the

[10] Returns here means excess of the increased revenue over the increased cost resulting from the investment (exclusive of the purchase price).

[11] As pointed out earlier, by using discounted rate of return instead of present value, the results are somewhat distorted. The same conclusions hold, however, and we feel that the discounted rate of return is conceptually simpler.

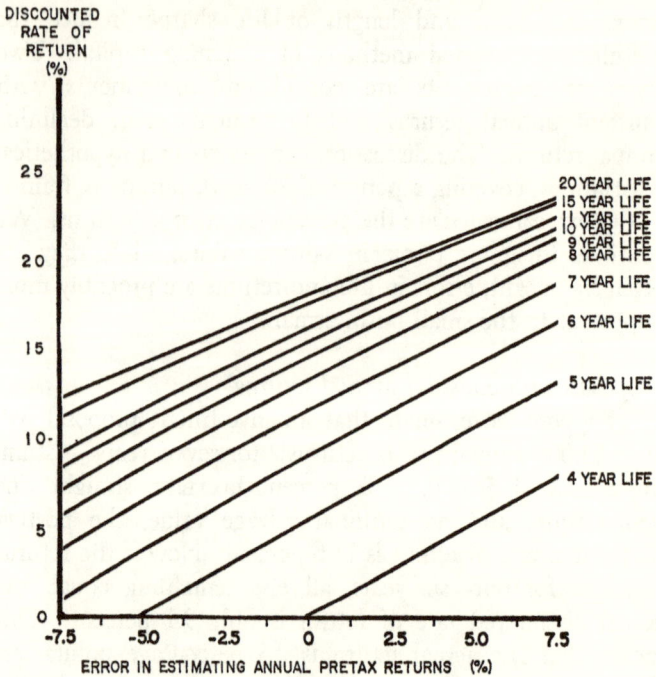

FIGURE 6-2

THE EFFECT OF ESTIMATING ERRORS (AS A PERCENTAGE OF
ORIGINAL INVESTMENT) ON THE DISCOUNTED RATE OF
RETURN—CONSTANT ANNUAL PRETAX RETURNS

original investment (2.5 percent error equals $100 in this
case). The line labeled "7 years" shows the discounted rates
of return for all investments with a life of seven years. As
the actual pretax returns decrease (negative estimating error
increases), the discounted rate of return declines. For this
reason the lines slope downward to the left.

In evaluating the effect of uncertainty, we can use
Figure 6-2 to determine the resulting variation in the
discounted rate of return with varying amounts of error in
estimation. The data used to construct Figure 6-2 are shown
in Table 6-2. Earlier, we said quite subjectively that a 5 to
10 percent error in annual pretax profits (as a percentage of

the original investment) would not seem improbable in the cases discussed. How much variation in the discounted rate of return could we expect with this amount of error? Suppose that an investment will actually return $1,000 annual pretax returns for seven years. If the estimated returns are subject to an error of plus or minus 2.5 percent and plus or minus one year, the maximum and minimum rates of return are 15.6 percent and 6.5 percent (as shown in Figure 6-2)—a variation of about nine percentage points. If we extend the possible error to plus or minus two years, the maximum and minimum rates are 16.8 percent and 2.8 percent, a variation of 14 percentage points. This magnitude of error in estimates seems likely to exist in practical decisions. This much uncertainty would probably discourage the use of theoretical rationing methods for ranking investment proposals. No significant difference may appear among proposals' rates of return if estimates are subject to this much error; and if the relative ranking of a group of investments is nearly obvious, alternative methods generally provide the same information with less cost.

Another interesting feature of Figure 6-2 is that it provides some insight into the effect of errors in length of life versus errors in returns. The relationship between errors of estimation in annual pretax returns and the discounted rate of return is almost linear, having a slope of about .021 to .026. This means that an error of about 2 to 2.5 percentage points in the discounted rate of return. This relationship is fairly constant throughout. On the other hand, the relationship between discounted rate of return and length of life is not linear. As the actual life decreases, an error of one year in the estimated life becomes more critical. The relationship is somewhat hyperbolic. When pretax profits equal $1,000 (zero error on horizontal axis) a five year difference in the length of life (between a life of 20 years and 15 years) results in less than one percentage point difference in the discounted rate of return. However, holding returns constant, a difference of only two years

71

## TABLE 6-2

### POSTTAX DISCOUNTED RATES OF RETURN FOR VARIOUS INVESTMENTS AND VARIOUS YEARS, WITH CONSTANT ANNUAL PRETAX RETURNS

| Annual pretax return<br>Life of proposal: | $700 | $750 | $800 | $850 | $900 | $950 | $1,000 | $1,050 | $1,100 | $1,150 | $1,200 | $1,250 | $1,300 |
|---|---|---|---|---|---|---|---|---|---|---|---|---|---|
| 20 years | .122 | .132 | .142 | .151 | .161 | .170 | .180 | .189 | .198 | .207 | .216 | .225 | .234 |
| 15 " | .112 | .123 | .134 | .144 | .154 | .165 | .175 | .184 | .194 | .204 | .213 | .223 | .232 |
| 11 " | .092 | .104 | .116 | .127 | .139 | .150 | .161 | .172 | .182 | .193 | .203 | .213 | .223 |
| 10 " | .083 | .096 | .108 | .120 | .131 | .143 | .154 | .165 | .176 | .187 | .197 | .208 | .218 |
| 9 " | .072 | .085 | .097 | .110 | .122 | .134 | .145 | .156 | .168 | .179 | .190 | .200 | .211 |
| 8 " | .057 | .071 | .083 | .096 | .109 | .121 | .133 | .145 | .156 | .168 | .179 | .190 | .201 |
| 7 " | .037 | .051 | .065 | .078 | .091 | .103 | .116 | .128 | .140 | .152 | .163 | .175 | .186 |
| 6 " | .010 | .024 | .038 | .052 | .065 | .078 | .091 | .104 | .116 | .129 | .141 | .153 | .165 |
| 5 " | * | .010 | .010 | .015 | .028 | .042 | .055 | .068 | .081 | .094 | .107 | .119 | .131 |
| 4 " | * | * | * | * | * | * | .010 | .014 | .027 | .041 | .054 | .066 | .079 |
| 3 " | * | * | * | * | * | * | * | * | * | * | * | * | * |

* Indicates negative discounted rate of return.

(between a life of four and six years) results in a change of more than eight percentage points in the discounted rate of return. Perhaps this is a good reason for businessmen being particularly cautious when estimating length of life.

The conclusions here are the same as those discussed earlier in connection with Cases 1 and 2: The usefulness of theoretical rationing methods appears seriously limited when dealing with uncertainty.

*Proposal with declining annual returns*

To make the analysis more general, we include the case of declining annual returns. Suppose we estimate that over a period of seven years an $8,000 investment (with 32 percent tax rate, straight line depreciation, and no terminal salvage value) will return $2,000, $1,900, $1,800, $1,700, $1,600, $1,500, and $1,400 annually (before taxes). This investment is taken as the standard of comparison; in other words, if the investment actually returns $2,000, $1,900, . . . , and $1,400 for seven years, there is no error in our estimates. If however the investment actually returns $2,000, $1,900, . . . , and $1,500 for six years, there is no error in our estimates of returns but a —1.0 year error in the length of life estimate. If the investment actually returns $1,900, $1,800, . . . , and $1,300 for seven years, there is no error in our length of life estimate, but there is a —1.25 percent error in the estimate of pretax returns. (Error is measured as the percentage of original investment that the estimate of first year return deviates from the actual return.)

If we plot the error in pretax returns on the horizontal axis and the discounted rate of return on the vertical axis, we can draw curves relating the discounted rates of return to various errors in returns. This procedure is carried out for lives of 3, 4, 5, . . . 20 years as was done in Figure 6-2; the results are shown in Figure 6-3. Figures 6-2 and 6-3 are very much alike, and almost everything that has been said applies to both. The conclusions about uncertainty seem equally applicable to constant and declining return investments.

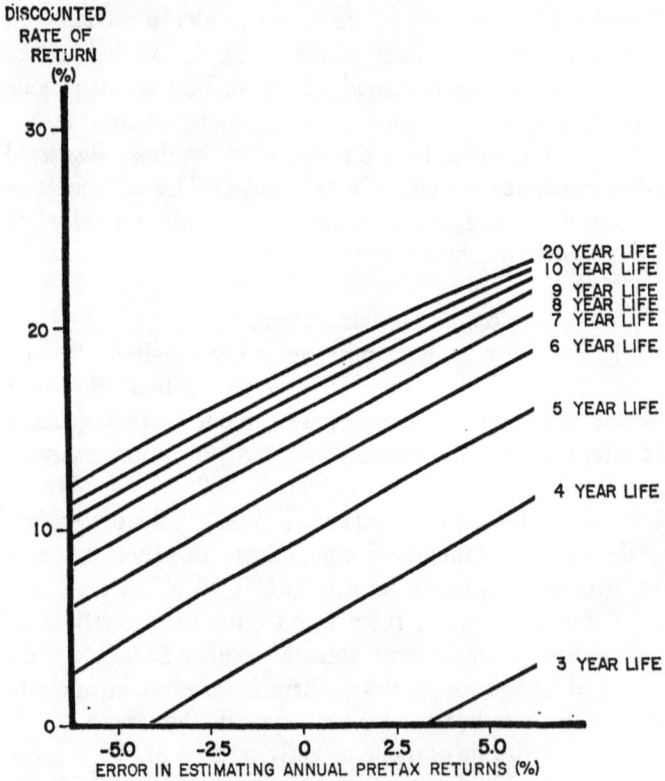

FIGURE 6-3

THE EFFECT OF ESTIMATING ERRORS (AS A PERCENTAGE OF
ORIGINAL INVESTMENT) ON THE DISCOUNTED RATE OF
RETURN—DECLINING ANNUAL PRETAX RETURNS

Unless an investment produces returns for an extremely
long period, a relatively small miscalculation in the estimate
of length of life (two to three years) can result in a drastic
overstatement of a proposal's profitability. Similarly a 2 to 5
percent overestimate of pretax returns can result in a serious
overstatement of profitability. Here, as with constant annual
returns, the relationship between errors in annual returns
and the discounted rate of return is almost linear, while the
relationship between errors in length of life and the dis-

counted rate of return is curvilinear; the errors in estimates of length of life become more important as actual life decreases.[12]

## The effect of technological change

Because the effects of errors in returns are linear and the effects of errors in life are curvilinear, errors in estimating annual returns may average out over a large number of investments, whereas errors in length of life will not. A two-year overestimate in length of life is not offset by a two-year underestimate on another comparable investment.

Today, with technological advancement so rapid and innovation so frequent, many capital investments are subject to an extremely high rate of obsolescence. Businessmen usually do not know which of their investments will be obsolete soon and are understandably worried about proposals that will take ten years to pay for themselves. The farther into the future one predicts, the more the uncertainty of obsolescence and the more unsure he is of the predictions.

By insisting on proposals that pay back quickly, within the realm of feasible prediction, the businessman is providing greater flexibility for himself. He is in a better position to maneuver and to change his plans when necessary.

Technological change is the main difficulty in estimating length of life. Businessmen can search for information about the expected returns in the early life of a proposal, but it is generally much more difficult to investigate expected returns late in the proposal's life. In addition, Figures 6-2 and 6-3 suggest that in many respects errors in length of life are more serious. Use of the short payback evades making estimates of returns in the later years and estimates of

---

[12] This curvilinear relationship is more apparent than real. The reason is that the discounted rate of return formula assumes that proceeds are reinvested at the resulting rate of return. Therefore, projects with higher rates of return possess a cumulative advantage in the formula but in the real world, reinvestment goes on regardless of the rate of the original investment.

length of life. The old saying about one bird in the hand being worth two in the bush is quite descriptive of business behavior in relation to the short payback period. It may be worthwhile to invest, receiving a small, quick return rather than to take a chance on a larger return with increased likelihood of obsolescence.

## SOME APPROACHES TO DECISION MAKING UNDER UNCERTAINTY

So far this chapter has centered on the ways in which uncertainty creates difficulties for the refined methods of investment analysis. But there has been no discussion of how to deal with the uncertainty itself. If there were some adequate method of dealing with uncertainty, refined analyses might be more useful. Let us now turn to four techniques publicized as possible aids in the problem of uncertainty.

### Subjective probability

Within recent years a new type of probability concept has appeared: personal or subjective probability. Savage is the best known advocate of this approach.[13] Personal probability is closely related to mathematical probability. Some writers have defined mathematical probability to be the relative frequency in the long run. Obviously if an event is unique or is about to occur for the first time, the concept of observing a very large number of trials is inapplicable. But people have degrees of belief about the future, and it is sometimes possible to quantify these beliefs in the form of subjective probabilities, although complicated problems arise in their empirical use. Following is an actual case illustration where subjective probabilities were quantified by a businessman.

Case 6. A small businessman was thinking about opening a branch store in a new shopping center. He could estimate

[13] L. J. Savage, Foundations of Statistics (New York: John Wiley and Sons, 1954).

most major costs and the investment necessary, but demand was uncertain. He stated that, in this case, market research appeared too costly. The businessman looked at the prospective location, talked to several associates, and computed a break-even point. He felt that his sales would exceed the break-even volume. The payback period was short, and so he decided to open the branch store. After he had made this decision and before it was completely implemented, he was asked to participate in an experiment designed to find out whether or not he could quantify his feelings about future sales. He stated the following: minimum weekly sales would amount to $500 per week; there was a 50 percent chance of selling $1,000 per week, a 30 percent chance of selling $1,500 per week, and a 20 percent chance of selling $2,000 per week.

If we calculate an expected value (or average), as is done with mathematical probabilities, we get $1,000 per week. The computation is shown below.

| $Amount = X$ | $Probability = P$ | $XP$ |
|---|---|---|
| 1st  $500 | 1.00 | $500 |
| 2nd $500 | .50 | 250 |
| 3rd  $500 | .30 | 150 |
| 4th  $500 | .20 | 100 |
| Expected value | | $1,000 |

The expected value could be looked upon as a *certainty equivalent*. In other words, we know that the future is uncertain but we might treat our average as if it were certain.

In the preceding example, the following monthly expenses were estimated.

| | |
|---|---|
| Rent | $200 |
| Advertising | 35 |
| Personnel | 190 |
| Utilities | 70 |
| TOTAL | $495 |

The cost of goods sold was estimated to be about 58 percent of sales, and the investment required for fixtures, working capital, and other equipment was estimated at $3,000. The owner felt that the store would continue for at least four to five years and perhaps much longer.

We can now perform the usual investment analysis outlined in Chapter 3. If we analyze the above incremental figures, we find that there is an expected pretax profit of about $16,000 annually. If we compute the present value or discounted rate of return for an investment of $3,000 returning $14,000 per year (before taxes) for five years or more, we find that this is obviously an extremely profitable investment.

This example illustrates the use of subjective or personal probabilities in uncertain situations. It is closely related to intuition or "hunch," but the results are more tangible and amenable to analysis. It should be remembered that subjective probabilities were quantified by the businessman in this illustration only after a request from the interviewer and after the actual decision was made. The acceptance of the investment proposal was based entirely on break-even and payback analysis. But behind this analysis the decision maker did think roughly in terms of the probabilities of being above or below the break-even point—he was almost certain that sales would be above it. Thus it appears that a crude subjective probability approach was used in the actual decision. Even if the manager were acquainted with probabilities, it was unnecessary for him to convert the probabilities into a certainty equivalent because of his high expectations of profitability.

### Minimax principle

What can we do when no reasonable estimate of probabilities can be made? One possible choice criterion is the minimax or maximin principle,[14] which attempts to maximize the minimum outcome. One interpretation of this states: FOR ALL POSSIBLE INVESTMENTS, CHOOSE THE ONE

[14] For a further discussion, see R. Duncan Luce and Howard Raiffa, *Games and Decisions* (New York: John Wiley and Sons, 1957), pp. 278-82.

WHICH HAS THE LOWEST MAXIMUM POSSIBLE COST OR THE HIGHEST MINIMUM POSSIBLE PROFIT. It is a pessimistic and conservative point of view. If one were to look upon investments as a game against nature and upon nature as a malevolent force, then the minimax principle would be the most sound. In Case 6, the owner had thought of another alternative: investing a comparable amount in a speculative stock. If he had applied the minimax principle to this situation, the obvious choice would have been to invest in the branch store because, as far as he was concerned, a profit on the store was assured whereas speculative stock could have resulted in a loss. One cannot determine whether he used the minimax principle; the investment proposal was apparently so profitable that the decision can be rationalized in terms of many different criteria. In fact, we cannot ascertain that the minimax principle was used in any of our investment case studies. Many businessmen are pessimistic, but this fact is not necessarily related to the minimax principle.

*Hurwicz principle*

When probabilities cannot be assessed and uncertainty exists, another principle of choice is the Hurwicz principle,[15] named after its originator. THE PROPER CHOICE IS THE PROPOSAL THAT MAXIMIZES THE WEIGHTED AVERAGE OF THE WORST AND BEST POSSIBLE OUTCOME; the weight used is a measure of the individual's pessimism or optimism ranging from zero to one.

To illustrate this principle let us look at another case.

*Case 7.* Mr. B, a small manufacturer of wood products, was having many of his parts made by a large lumber mill about 200 miles away. The reason for this arrangement was that Mr. B did not own the proper equipment to make these parts. On being notified of a small price increase on these parts, he began analyzing the feasibility of buying machinery to do the work in his own plant. One of Mr. B's products required that several

[15] See Luce and Raiffa, pp. 282-84.

pieces of lumber be cut to certain lengths and milled to desired specifications; precision was not very important. The pieces from the mill cost about 32 cents per foot, and Mr. B used two- and three-foot lengths about three inches wide. He could also use the scrap for hidden one-foot lengths. The machine to perform the necessary cutting would cost about $800; there was uncertainty, however, about the savings that would be produced. Rough lumber would cost $5.00 to $6.00 per hundred board feet; Mr. B figured that 50 percent of the rough lumber would be waste. Out of ten board feet, five were estimated to be usable, which means that the rough lumber would cost about 20 cents per usable foot. The other necessary milling and sanding would cost at least 3 cents and at most 5 cents. This meant a saving of from 7 cents to 9 cents per foot. The greatest amount of uncertainty existed in the number of feet that would be used. He placed a lower limit of 1,000 feet per year and an upper limit of 15,000 feet per year. The product was relatively new and sales data had not been collected. Even if they had been, there was no guarantee that past sales had any relationship to future sales.

The savings then would amount to between $70 and $1,350 per year. If we simply depreciate the machine over a three year period (using the depreciation as an expense), in three years the incremental profit could be as much as $3,250 or the incremental loss as much as $590. The information is placed in a matrix below. $S_0$ means the worst future, $S_1$ the best future. Figures are profit or loss.

| Alternative | $S_0$ | $S_1$ |
|---|---|---|
| buy machine | −$590 | +$3,250 |
| do not buy | 0 | 0 |

The minimax principle would say that the machine should not be bought. The choice using the Hurwicz principle depends upon Mr. B's degree of optimism, which can range from zero to one and will be called $a$. The Hurwicz Criterion is computed as $S_1(a) + S_0(1 - a)$. If Mr. B is very pessimistic $(a = 0)$, then the Hurwicz Criterion is the same as the minimax principle. We shall compute the "value" of the machine for different degrees of optimism.

| Alpha | Value |
|-------|-------|
| .1 | —$206 |
| .3 | 562 |
| .5 | 1,330 |
| .7 | 2,098 |
| .9 | 2,866 |

The value of not buying the machine is zero for any value of $a$. If Mr. B. is at all optimistic, he would buy the machine using the Hurwicz Criterion.

It should be clear that there is no evidence that Mr. B did in fact apply the Hurwicz Criterion. The case has been used to illustrate how the criterion might be applied. Mr. B did buy the machine, but it is difficult to determine the mental processes that took place.[16]

### Laplace principle

It may seem strange and unbusinesslike to use only the best and worst outcomes in the analysis. The Laplace principle[17] takes all possible futures into account. This principle states that IF NO PROBABILITIES CAN BE ASSESSED, THEN TREAT EACH FUTURE AS IF IT WERE EQUIPROBABLE. If only two futures are possible in the above example, this would coincide with the Hurwicz principle for $a = .5$; but in fact many futures are possible. In Case 7, a multitude of possibilities exist; let us, for example, list seven possibilities. The numbers represent profits.

| Alternative | $S_0$ | $S_1$ | $S_2$ | $S_3$ | $S_4$ | $S_5$ | $S_6$ |
|-------------|-------|-------|-------|-------|-------|-------|-------|
| buy machine | —$590 | —$50 | $590 | $1,230 | $1,870 | $2,510 | $3,250 |
| do not buy | 0 | 0 | 0 | 0 | 0 | 0 | 0 |

If we assume that each future has a one-seventh chance of occurring, the expected value of buying the machine would

[16] Mr. B decided it was very likely that he would continue to have a need for this machine in other types of products. He also felt that the product in question had great sales potential and that his sales would increase during the next year.

[17] See Luce and Raiffa, pp. 284-86.

be $1,244, opposed to an expected value of zero for not buying the machine.

*Usefulness of these principles*

There are other principles of decision under uncertainty, but they will not be discussed here. The Minimax, Hurwicz, and Laplace principles assume that the decision maker has no reason to think any one future is more probable than another.[18] Every case in this project involved some *degree of belief* about particular futures. Some futures may have been considered equiprobable by the decision makers, but there were always some futures that were looked upon as less or more likely than others. It would seem that the Laplace, Hurwicz, and Minimax principles have little to offer in actual decisions because the environment of uncertainty assumed apparently does not exist. Businessmen are not completely ignorant of the future. They have some definite ideas as to likely and unlikely futures, and therefore the Laplace, Hurwicz, and Minimax principles are inapplicable. Of the methods discussed, the use of subjective probabilities appears to have the most relevance to and most usefulness in the capital investment decisions studied.

The subjective probability approach requires further attention. Even though an entrepreneur may have strong or weak feelings about the occurrence of a future, he may not be able to quantify this feeling into a probability measure. Even if a businessman could quantify these beliefs, he may not be willing to gamble on the expected value as a certainty equivalent.

Case 6 of this chapter related an actual example in

[18] Some authors would disagree with this statement. Disagreement is found in David W. Miller and Martin K. Starr, *Executive Decisions and Operations Research* (Englewood Cliffs, N. J.: Prentice-Hall, 1960), p. 94. The Minimax and Hurwicz outcomes are entirely independent of the particular future, such as war or peace. The choice depends only upon the largest and/or smallest payoffs *regardless of the future they represent.* The choice depends purely upon blind optimism or blind pessimism or some combination of the two, but not on a specific future event.

which a small businessman did predict, in probability terms, sales for an entirely new operation with no more than qualitative information about sales potential. The probability estimates given by him were shown to yield an average (or expected) sales figure of $1,000 per week. He stated, before making the estimates, that the figures would be "pretty far off."

Even if one accepts the subjective probability approach as a description of actual behavior in the face of uncertainty, it is still doubtful that the decision maker thinks in terms of the entire probability distribution or converts it into a certainty equivalent. Instead of analyzing an entire continuous range of outcomes, the decision maker probably focuses attention on a few of special interest. Shackle suggests that decision makers concentrate on two outcomes: a focus gain and a focus loss.[19] This may be more realistic than to describe the manager as thinking in terms of an entire distribution, but it also seems an oversimplification. Some businessmen may concentrate on three, four, or more outcomes; there is no reason to accept two as the magic number. But the point is that the decision maker necessarily simplifies the problem by considering only part of the possibility set. Then it seems reasonable to suppose that he attaches rough subjective probabilities to these two, three, or four outcomes and decides on this basis (as in Case 1).

If the decision maker does focus attention on a few outcomes, it may be unnecessary to convert them into expected values or averages, especially if all the outcomes are favorable (as in Case 6). Furthermore the averaging process obscures the amount of variance among the outcomes, and this variance could well influence the decision. As Hart has suggested, no certainty equivalent can take the place of a range of subjective probabilities.[20]

[19] G. L. S. Shackle, *Expectations in Economics* (Cambridge: Cambridge University Press, 1949).

[20] A. G. Hart, "Anticipations, Uncertainty and Dynamic Planning," *Journal of Business*, XIII (October 1940, part 2), *University of Chicago Studies in Business Administration*, vol. XI, no. 1.

Expected value techniques in which subjective probabilities are taken into account may be useful; or they may not be palatable to the decision maker. Small businessmen, whose capital is limited, cannot always afford to gamble on the basis of averages or expected values, because, if they lose, bankruptcy may ensue. Therefore gains and losses of the same magnitude are probably not equally advantageous or disadvantageous. When the investment involves large sums of money and large possible gains and losses, the small businessman may feel the greatest need for careful analysis. but certainty equivalents, rather than filling this need, would simply confuse the issue.[21] The variance may be as important as the mean. Also, as was pointed out earlier, negative deviations in length of life are more unprofitable to the firm than positive deviations are profitable.

Perhaps it would be useful to distinguish between two subjective probability approaches. One is nonquantitative, and involves very rough evaluations of outcomes in terms of "likely," "very likely," and so on. The other involves an attempt to quantify the likelihoods and to analyze them systematically. Many small businesses may now use the first approach (as in Cases 1 and 6). The issue is whether they should be encouraged to quantify their expectations.

One slightly different variant of subjective probability is what has been called the *most probable future*.[22] The decision maker considers only one possible future, the most probable one, and treats it as if it were certain to occur. This technique, although widely used, is simply another expression of personal judgment. It is less complete than subjective probabilities, and the same difficulties arise.

[21] Robert Schlaifer, *Probability and Statistics for Business Decisions* (New York: McGraw-Hill Book Company, 1959), pp. 24-48. Although these ideas are not original with Schlaifer, he presents an excellent discussion.

[22] William T. Morris, *Engineering Economy* (Homewood, Ill.: Richard D. Irwin, 1960), p. 213. Morris uses this technique in a little different sense, since he calls it a principle of choice under risk, where subjective probabilities are irrelevant.

A review of some suggested methods of analysis under uncertainty has revealed little that can be classified as useful to the practical businessman except a nonanalytical tool called judgment. This being the case, let us return to the chief tool with which the small businessman analyzes the investment problem under uncertainty: the payback period.

## THE PAYBACK PERIOD: A RATIONALE

*Most* authors who have written on the subject of capital budgeting have denied that the payback period is a sound approach to the rationing of capital. Gordon has shown (see p. 22) that in some cases the payback reciprocal is an excellent estimate of the discounted rate of return and that the use of the payback period or payback reciprocal is justified. In Chapter 4 we have shown that while what Gordon says is true, the payback reciprocal is unreliable when used as a measure of *relative* profitability among investment proposals. One might then conclude that the payback period is of little use in investment analysis.

In Chapter 5 we related several studies of business practice. Overwhelmingly, the most popular rationing formula is the payback period. We also found this to be true in small businesses. Why then is this the case? If the payback period is so unreliable, why is its use so prevalent? Our answer is that its use is *not* unsound in the majority of cases studied, notwithstanding what was said earlier. As the first step in supporting our point, let us assume that a decision maker, trying to decide whether to open a branch store, applies break-even analysis. He gathers estimates of variable and fixed cost and plots them on a chart, similar to Figure 6-4. He now sees that (within certain assumptions) if sales exceed 15,000 units, the new store will be profitable.

The businessman makes use of this type of analysis because of uncertainty. He might not have any exact probability measures of future sales, but he will most likely possess strong feelings concerning the likelihood of selling a

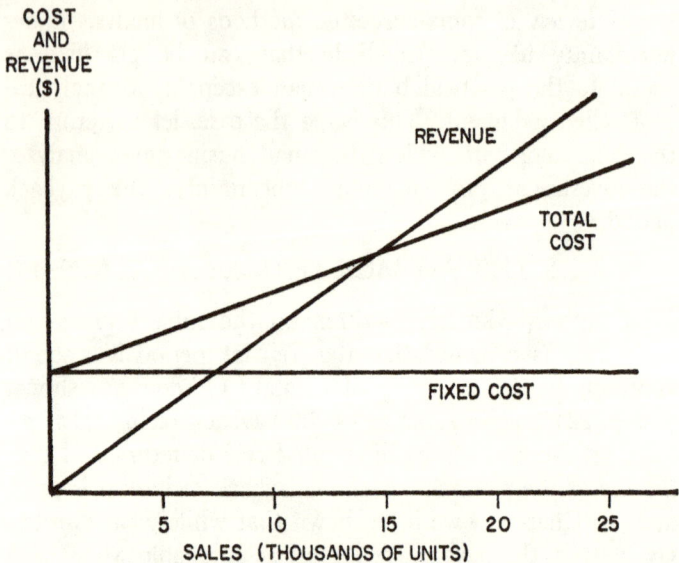

COST AND REVENUE ($)

REVENUE

TOTAL COST

FIXED COST

SALES (THOUSANDS OF UNITS)

FIGURE 6-4
BREAK-EVEN CHART

particular amount. The greater the uncertainty, however, the more nebulous will be his feelings and the more difficult it will be to quantify them.

It is important to note that in break-even analysis, the only independent variable is output or sales, profit being the dependent variable (the result of changes in output). Costs are taken as known.

In capital investment decisions, very often two *principal* uncertain factors occur—annual income and length of life of the investment. An error in either or both of these can lead to unprofitable investments. The following sections attempt to demonstrate that the payback approach is analogous to break-even analysis and serves the same function in the treatment of uncertainty. The argument falls into three sections: (a) when returns are uncertain but the life is certain; (b) when the returns are certain but the life is uncertain; and (c) when both are uncertain.

*Certain life or long-lived investments with returns uncertain*

When the useful life of a proposal is certain or very long, say 20 to 30 years, then errors in this variable (life) become less important. For example, if obsolescence occurs after the twentieth year, it may produce only a slightly less profitable investment than if obsolescence occurs after the twenty-fifth year.[23] In this case, break-even analysis may be completely justified. If total fixed costs and unit variable costs are fairly certain, variations in sales are generally the most important uncertain factor. Through break-even charts one may be able to ascertain the sales volume necessary to avoid unprofitability. This is the type of analysis that was actually used in Case 2. Although there the life was not known, four years was considered to be the absolute minimum life. If the life of a proposal is long, then the break-even chart shows approximate profits for each time period over a long period of time. If the life is fairly certain, a determination of the profitability can be made. But if the life is uncertain, even after conventional break-even analysis, the proposal's profitability is dubious; the businessman does not know if his original investment will be returned. For this reason, we say that investments with known life or long life can often be analyzed using break-even charts.

*Returns known with life uncertain*

This situation is quite typical of many laborsaving investments. It is also indicative, in a limited sense, of many other investment proposals that we have studied through interviews with small businessmen. For example, a businessman may know, with almost complete certainty, how much a new machine will save annually. He may not know how long the product will be marketable or when better equipment will be available. He may not even be sure of the machine's physical life. The analysis of this case involves

[23] The reason for this is that returns far in the future are discounted quite heavily. This discounting is, of course, heavier for higher interest rates.

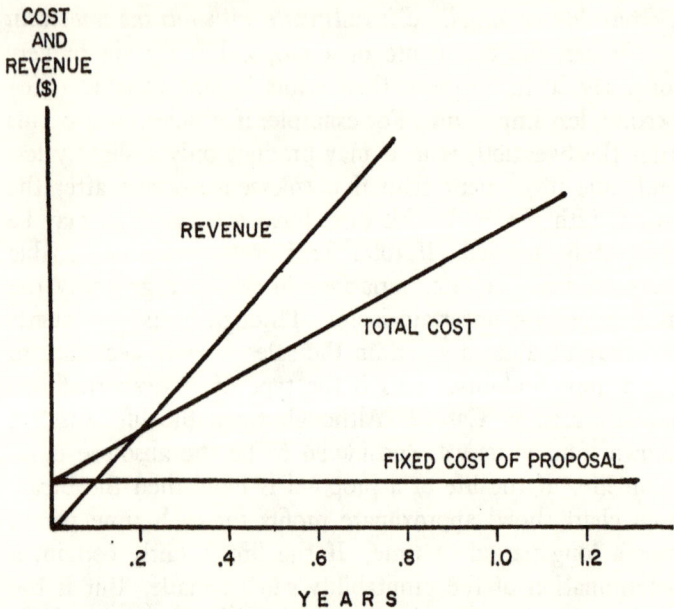

FIGURE 6-5
INVESTMENT BREAK-EVEN CHART

a different type of break-even chart. This chart is similar to the conventional break-even chart; however, time is plotted on the horizontal axis. In Case 6, the small businessman might have proceeded by using the following analysis.[24]

Expected sales are $52,000 per year; expected expenses are $5,940 per year plus 58 percent of sales (totaling $36,100 annual expenses). Initial cost of the proposed investment is $3,000. This information is shown in Figure 6-5. We can see that the break-even point is less than one year. The rate of discounting and obsolescence creates inaccuracies; the higher the rate, the more inaccurate are the results.

Figure 6-5 is nothing more than a refinement of the payback period. It tells us at approximately what length of

[24] Since the owner had very definite ideas about length of life, this illustration does not meet all the requirements of the section.

life of the investment profitability will begin. This is the same information given by the payback period, which can be computed as $3,000/$15,900 = .2 years. A little more information is given in Figure 6-5, such as approximate pretax profits if the investment lasts three or four years, etc. There are, of course, conceptual differences between Figures 6-4 and 6-5, but they are relatively unimportant here. The point to be made is that in a situation such as this, where annual returns are known (or where a certainty equivalent is used) and length of life is unknown, the payback period may be a useful tool of analysis. After it is found, the decision maker can ask himself whether he believes that the life will be longer than the payback period. If so, it may be a profitable investment. In this way he is using the non-quantitative type of subjective probabilities.

*Case* 8. One of the largest manufacturers of typewriters in the world uses the payback period in investment decisions. If a piece of special purpose equipment is proposed, it must be able to pay for itself in at least two years. If general purpose machinery is proposed, it must pay back in at least five years.

The high rate of technological change in this industry is a chief factor influencing this policy. Even large firms are found to use the payback period as a criterion, and although this method may not be optimum, it seems to be satisfactory.

*Length of life and returns unknown*

This situation is typical of many investment proposals at their very beginnings. Naturally, the more search for information, the less uncertain becomes the length of life and returns. There is no sharp dividing line between the known and unknown. Actually, most decisions are made with information that is somewhere between these two extremes.

*Case* 9. A small trucking firm has been toying with the idea of installing two-way radios in each of 11 trucks. The truck routes extend from 10 to 50 miles from the central office. Many advantages have been brought out in favor of radios, but as yet, no solid dollars and cents figures exist. A trade publication article claims that one company saved the cost of its radios in two years. This article has stimulated management thinking somewhat; no action has been taken.

What is the result of this great uncertainty? In Case 9, the investment decision was postponed until more information was available. Few proposals involving so much uncertainty are accepted unless great profitability is obvious at the outset or some predetermined commitment or judgment has been made. This point is extremely important in the explanation of the sequential nature of investment decisions brought about by uncertainty.

## Sequential decisions

Investment analysis results in three types of action concerning proposals: they are accepted, rejected, or held for further study. Many proposals that we studied remained in the third state for a considerable length of time. It seems important to distinguish between a proposal that has been rejected and one that is being held—not necessarily studied. One method of relieving uncertainty about the future is simply to wait until the future arrives. Sometimes immediate decisions (and therefore predictions) are necessary. In the actual cases in this study, when the uncertainty was great and the decision was postponable, our subjects have generally chosen to push the decision into the future until more information was at hand. This sometimes led to search for new alternatives or information, the subject of the next chapter.

## CONCLUSION

*Theoretical* methods of investment evaluation (present value and discounted rate of return) assume decision making under conditions of certainty. Usual business investments are not made under these conditions. Because some alternative methods are fairly accurate estimates of the discounted rate of return and because some of them can rank proposals quite well, there is reason for substituting these alternative methods for those that are theoretically more accurate. Also, if uncertainty is so great that satisfactory predictions are not possible, no logical or mathematical significance may emerge in the results of theoretical methods.

Few businessmen, especially small businessmen, would be willing to predict the future outcome of an investment for more than a few years. Consequently, they are generally unwilling to invest when the profitability depends upon years beyond the prediction period. A break-even point of profitability is determined, the payback period. If it is strongly felt that the proposal will continue its returns for at least this time, the proposal may be accepted. The results are similar to a "go-no-go" gauge. Perhaps this is altogether satisfactory for the small businessman in our present state of knowledge.

A point that has been postponed until now concerns businessmen's objectives. If profit maximization is not the sole goal of the decision maker, then so-called theoretical methods of evaluation are not optimum unless or until utility is measurable. The subjective methods of the businessman facilitate the evaluation of objectives such as security, ethics, and personal satisfaction better than any mathematical formulation. It is generally agreed, and our interviews indicate, that businessmen have multiple objectives, one of which is *satisfactory* profits. Judgment, combined with alternative rationing methods, may be quite adequate in achieving these objectives.

We have tried to build some arguments for the use of alternative rationing formulas. Traditional literature on the subject of capital budgeting in America seems to overstress decision making under certainty and neglects the practical businessman whose world is far from certain. Instead of placing so much emphasis on refined rationing techniques, we believe that stress on other important areas, such as search, will yield higher marginal productivity.

A possible aid to theoretical methods is the development of low cost computer installations. With lightning-fast speed these electronic mechanisms calculate data that can prove extremely helpful in investment decisions. Some computer programs have already been written that include reasoning on the basis of probability and other features.[25] These computers are still beyond the financial capabilities of most small firms, and even if they were available, there is serious question as to their practicality: the processing cost is only one cost; time and training are also required for such facilities. In the final analysis, because of uncertainty about the future, judgment remains the most important factor in capital budgeting.

Until forecasting techniques become more accurate and less expensive, the payback period and other alternative methods will probably remain a primary tool of practical capital investment analysis and refined methods will continue to be little used and little understood, particularly in small business.

[25] For example, see Roger Orensteen and Ron Cummings, *A Capital Investment Program for the* IBM *1620* (Chicago: International Business Machines, 1960).

# 7

## SEARCH ACTIVITY IN
## INVESTMENT DECISIONS

$\mathcal{I}$N MAKING investment decisions in small business, a critical consideration is sometimes the search function. Of the many possible types of search activity the investor is most actively engaged in seeking *alternatives* and in seeking *information*. Both of these types, of course, are closely associated with the function of evaluation.

### PROGRAMED AND NONPROGRAMED ASPECTS

A *completely* programed decision involves a routine procedure in which each step of the decision-making process is specified beforehand. This does not imply that the conclusion is predetermined, only the procedure. It is analogous to a computer program designed to solve some problem, each step of the program being specified. For example, a computer can be instructed to decide which of two numbers is the larger. We would write a series of instructions to solve the problem. They might be: (a) locate the first number; (b) locate the second number; (c) subtract the first number from the second number; (d) if the answer is negative, choose the first number; if it is positive, choose the second; and (e) print the larger number. The beauty of a completely specified program is that it can be repeated.

A completely nonprogramed approach implies that no systematic routine whatsoever is determined beforehand. It requires intermediate decisions about each succeeding step in the whole process.

Most investment decision processes fall somewhere between these two extremes. Some portions of the decision are routinized, but others are not. We henceforth use the words programed and nonprogramed to refer to the predominance of routinization or lack of it. If a decision process is highly routinized, it is called a programed decision; if not, it is called nonprogramed.

Search activity, too, can be programed or nonprogramed. A computer can be programed to search a table or numbers for the smallest. This is programed search. On the other hand, nonprogramed search occurs if a child hunts for the smallest number in a completely disorganized way; or if an entrepreneur—after looking at his financial statement—decides that profits are much too low and looks for the cause without any plan. If this happens often, some routine usually results as a matter of habit.

In order to clarify the discussion that follows, it is necessary to make still another distinction: that between *planned* and *spontaneous* search activity. Planned search is the result of setting aside a portion of someone's time for the explicit purpose of performing search activity. The distinguishing aspect is that the time is apportioned before the problem arises. Spontaneous search may also result in rationing of time, but it is not performed until a problem is encountered. For purposes of clarity, the two kinds are summarized below in Table 7-1.

TABLE 7-1

CLASSIFICATIONS OF SEARCH ACTIVITY

|  | Planned | Spontaneous |
|---|---|---|
| Nonprogramed | Routine; formulated to use for any applicable problem; takes place at a planned time. | Routine; formulated to use for any applicable problem; takes place only when search is deemed necessary because a problem arises. |
| Programmed | Without a predetermined routine; may be disorganized or proceed helter-skelter; performed at a preplanned time. | Without a predetermined routine; may be disorganized; applicable to and performed only after a specific problem arises. |

## SEARCH ACTIVITY FOUND IN THE CASE STUDIES

*The purpose* of this section is to describe the types of search activity found in our case studies[1] and the motivation involved. First, three cases are discussed which give little attention to search in investment decisions. They represent the great majority of cases gathered in our study. Next, three other cases are discussed in which extraordinary attention seems to have been given to search. Later in the chapter an evaluation is attempted.

[1] Detailed discussions of the cases in this chapter are found in Appendix C.

*Dry cleaner case*

Mr. E, a dry cleaner, had an opportunity to open a branch dry cleaning store in a new shopping center. After looking at the center, talking to associates, and computing a break-even point, he decided to invest. His demand estimate was based on information given to him by the promoter of the shopping center.

The search for information was both spontaneous and nonprogramed. Mr. E had no predetermined approach to the collection of data. He devoted little time to finding sources of information for demand estimates, such as city planning and zoning maps of population. He had no time for such things because of involvement in the day-to-day details of his business. He did not delegate many routine tasks in maintenance, collections, and deliveries.

Similarly, the search for alternatives was neither planned nor programed. Mr. E did consider the possible purchase of common stock as an alternative to opening the branch store, but the search went no further. Instead of seeking out still other alternatives, he considered only proposals brought to his attention; this was true of the branch store proposal itself. The issue in this case is whether the delegation of routine tasks would have profited Mr. E by providing him with time for more concentrated attention to investment alternatives.

*Wearing apparel case* A

The engineering department of this firm is capable of making cost and revenue estimates for investment analysis. The company, however, seldom calls on the engineering department for this purpose. In one specific decision concerning a proposed merger, a quick look at the financial statement concluded the decision-making process. No analysis of cost and revenue allocations was made; only net profit was of interest. Mr. F, the president, was concerned primarily with sales; his daily schedule was built around sales activities, leaving little time to examine the proposed merger. A decision to build a new plant was handled in a similar manner. The only real search undertaken concerned the availability of necessary funds.

By the president's own admission, "Only one investment opportunity seems to come up at a time." In other words, no search for alternative investment proposals is undertaken. When proposals do appear, they are presented to the firm by some outsider. The net result is that when a proposal is evaluated, the president has few if any other investment opportunities with which to compare it. Projects are evaluated on their absolute merits according to a one-year payback criterion. The president could not explain the reasoning behind this policy; he simply stated that it seemed to work. Surely if active search effort were initiated, many profitable investments could be discovered, if only internal improvements. The engineering department could investigate materials handling efficiency, purchase quantities, and a host of other improvements requiring investment.

*Wearing apparel case B*

This case is very similar to wearing apparel case A. Mr. G has little time for the analysis of investment decisions. Sales are his primary interest. A proposal for the purchase of new typewriters was so clearly profitable that little search for information was needed (assuming that the salesman's estimates of savings could be trusted).

The company was involved in few investment decisions. This fact reflects the absence of search for alternatives and furnishes another example of an executive so completely submerged in other aspects of his business that he has no time for search activity.

These three cases indicate a pattern found in the majority of our case studies. The decision maker has not planned to search for information or alternatives. As a result, each investment decision is made suddenly. Time is limited and usually a hurried decision is necessary.

We now turn to cases in which planned search activity

leads to a wider range of alternatives, more information, and avoidance of decisions under pressure.

*Coin-operated laundry case*

In this case, Mr. X evaluated at least three investment proposals. These were the creation of a stock investment company, purchase of real estate for rental purposes, and establishment of a coin-operated laundry. Mr. X specified three criteria for choice: (a) a cash outlay not to exceed $6,000; (b) little time required out of Mr. X's daily routine; and (c) a cash investment payback period not to exceed three to three and one-half years. These prior conditions were not inflexible; in fact, the first condition was violated when a $15,000 cash outlay was finally accepted. Such criteria did serve as tentative decision rules, eliminating from consideration clearly unacceptable alternatives.

A realization of excess cash on hand intensified Mr. X's search activity. After examination of all three proposals, he chose the one that seemed most satisfactory—investment in the coin laundry. He then spent his time and effort on transforming the idea into "brick and mortar." He discontinued the search for additional investments because he had committed his cash reserve and had no additional time for search.

The search for information was simultaneous with the evaluation of the three proposals. As soon as an alternative was deemed unsatisfactory, no further information was sought. When it was discovered that the stock investment company proposal required too much time and cash, it was discarded. When it appeared that the rental property proposal would provide too little cash return in the early years, search ended. Most of the search for information concerned the laundry proposal. At first the stress was on information about profitability; this ended when the proposal was accepted. Then the stress was laid upon information about maintenance characteristics of the equipment, store layout, and the like. Thus the search was intensified when a proposal appeared acceptable and halted when the proposal seemed unacceptable, a pattern opposite to that in the search for alternatives. Rejection of a proposal leads to the search for other alternatives; acceptance leads to greater stress on the search for information.

Why did Mr. X devote so much attention to search activity? He had a driving ambition to retire at an early age. He wished to invest heavily in his early years, so that he could later live comfortably on the returns. Accordingly, he adopted a reasonable pattern of search activity, consisting of (a) delegation of routine work to provide time for investment analysis; (b) simultaneous consideration of several investment proposals instead of just one at a time as is usual among small firms; and (c) expansion of search activity when it seemed profitable, curtailment when it seemed unnecessary, with appropriate shifts between the search for alternatives and the search for information.

Mr. X's search activity was planned but not programed. It was flexible enough to permit concentrated effort where effort produced results.

*Wholesale liquor dealer case*

Mr. D devotes most of his time to the search for alternatives and information. After years of routine work, he decided that he was not moving forward. Accordingly, he hired a sales manager at $10,000 per year to relieve him of the routine work and turned to larger matters.

The search for alternatives in his case is rather unusual. Mr. D keeps a file of ideas for investments. Periodically he reviews the contents, updating any previous information and adding new schemes that are conceived in the meantime. In this manner he continuously evaluates alternatives. When a new problem arises, he has time to work toward a solution. If it has come up before, he looks into the file and begins where he left off in the analysis. His time is quite flexible, a fact which enables him to attack any important or urgent problem. Some investments are obviously inferior to those in the idea file, and they are at once discarded. Others are apparently better than any in the file, and he searches further to find out whether they are really superior. If other plans are more pressing, the ideas go into the file and are re-searched at some other time.

Because he is constantly searching for new and better investments, evaluation of any one proposal is thus made much simpler. Even though the final choice is based on rather unsophisticated methods, it is probably a sound one because it is deemed better than any of the backlog of other seemingly profitable proposals. Any of Mr. D's actual investments can be counted on to be very profitable.

Search for information is also quite important in this case. Mr. D has time to perform this search and does not have to rely upon a salesman's figures or a hunch with no logical basis. When a salesman told him that electronic data processing equipment would pay great dividends and even presented dollars and cents advantages, Mr. D was able to find out for himself. By talking to associates in a firm of similar size in the same business, he could get a better idea of how the equipment would actually perform. Through imaginative search he found out that the equipment was probably not suited to his particular firm.

Perhaps some of Mr. D's success at search stems from the fact that he is adventurous. His investment in direct telephones to another city is undoubtedly sound for his industry, though it could prove unsuccessful. Although he has hedged the investment somewhat (the telephone con-tract can be discontinued at any time), the chances of success seem good. Mr. D's interviewing many retailers in this town convinced him that increased profits will result. Adventurous as he is, he never makes an investment without an investigation of the situation.

We contend that Mr. D's ability to size up these situations is due to experience and a fine backlog of possible investment proposals without the pressure of time to force decisions based on scanty facts.

*Food products company case*

This firm differs from most of the firms in our study. It is larger (with about 200 employees) and attracts nationwide customers. Although the management seems to give almost no conscious effort to search for alternatives, there is always a large backlog of projects. Department heads and foremen periodically submit a large number of investment proposals. Istvan,[2] who studied 48 very large firms, found the same situation in his studies. He found only one large firm making a special effort to search for alternative investment proposals. This seems to be the most glaring difference between big business and small business in the investment decision-making process; large firms accumulate a wealth of proposals without much effort, whereas small firms must search for them vigorously if they want to build up a backlog of opportunities from which to choose when the occasion for investment arises.

In this firm a postaudit of completed and active proposals is undertaken each year. Estimates are checked against actual results; the responsible party must defend his estimates if discrepancies exist. No other firm covered by this study performs a formal, planned postaudit. This may again be due to the size of the firm. Very small businessmen may have less need for formal postaudit because they are personally responsible for each investment decision. In large firms, the decision makers and the initiators of proposals are generally not the same people. The postaudit serves as both a control and an information device, neither of which is needed by all small businessmen in their investment decisions.

## THE MARCH-SIMON SEARCH HYPOTHESES

*As background* for the evaluation of the cases just discussed, we introduce three hypotheses outlined by March and

[2] Istvan, p. 46.

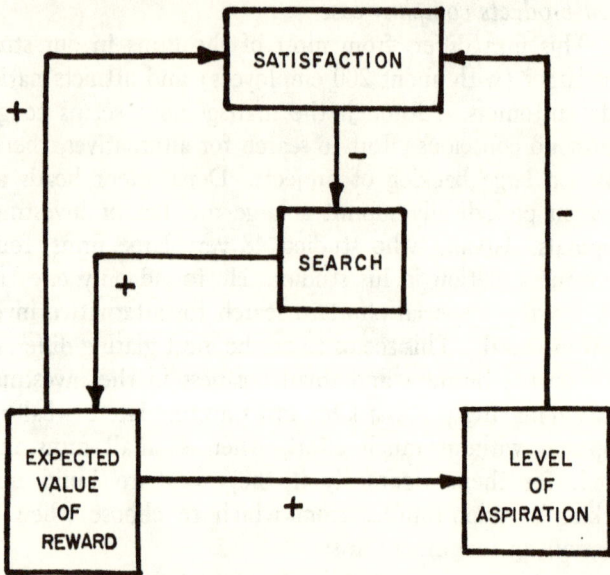

FIGURE 7-1

GENERAL MODEL OF ADAPTIVE MOTIVATED BEHAVIOR

Simon.[3] This section lays a theoretical framework for the remainder of the chapter.

*General model of adaptive motivated behavior*

The March-Simon model of adaptive motivated behavior is reproduced in Figure 7-1. Quite simply the model says that search activity is a result of dissatisfaction.[4] The higher the dissatisfaction, the more search for alternatives will take place. The more search, the higher the expected value of the reward. The higher the expected value, the higher the satisfaction and aspiration level. The higher the aspiration level, the lower the satisfaction. The following discussion

[3] J. G. March and H. A. Simon, *Organizations* (New York: John Wiley and Sons, 1958), pp. 48, 116, 185.

[4] The description here is a gross oversimplification and ignores some qualifications.

examines several cases and the relationship between actual search behavior and the general model of adaptive behavior.

*Empirical search for alternatives and the general hypothesis*[5]

Search for alternatives actually does appear to stem from dissatisfaction. In the automatic coin laundry case, Mr. X was dissatisfied with a 4 or 5 percent return and started looking for more lucrative investments. This could easily have resulted from an upward shift in, or an already high level of, aspiration. Mr. X stated that his objective was to retire comfortably at an early age.

In the wholesale liquor dealer case, dissatisfaction with profits and progress was certainly responsible for a major portion of the search for alternatives. Mr. D's aspiration level appears quite high and is still rising. This same reasoning would also hold for the billboard company and the vending machine company, cited in the appendix.

In the dry cleaner case and the two wearing apparel cases, the aspiration levels of the managers seem to be as high as in other cases, but search for alternative investment opportunities does not result. According to the general hypothesis, search should occur; it probably does, but in other areas of the firm, such as sales. Therefore, these cases neither confirm nor refute the hypothesis.

*Empirical search for information and the general hypothesis*

Search for information seems to be motivated in quite a different manner from search for alternatives. When a businessman believes that an alternative is worth considering, search for information begins. Search in this case is motivated by the satisfaction of finding a workable alternative. When an alternative seems unsatisfactory, the small businessman discontinues his search for information. In this case dissatisfaction curtails search activity. It is true that as the collection of information proceeds, the project may

[5] General hypothesis is synonymous with general model of adaptive motivated behavior.

appear unrewarding, leading to dissatisfaction and a new search for alternatives; but search for information seems to be motivated by satisfaction rather than dissatisfaction.

These statements are borne out by the cases in this chapter. Therefore, we conclude that the general hypothesis is more applicable to search for alternatives than to search for information.[6]

## Time pressure hypothesis

According to March and Simon, time pressure and stress have two effects: (a) search (for some individuals) becomes less fruitful; and (b) although the rate of search may increase and become vigorous, it is largely stereotyped.

The second portion of this hypothesis is not supported by our case studies. Some of the decisions were made hastily because of time pressures, but the vigor of search was not increased.[7] In fact, in some cases time pressure precluded search. In wearing apparel case A, the president's time was scarce because he attended to so many of the company's sales details. When the prospect of a merger presented itself, he quickly rejected the proposal. In the dry cleaning case, Mr. E did not look into demand very deeply because his available time was limited and he was under the pressure of routine details.

The first part of the hypothesis relating to less fruitful search due to stress and time pressure is upheld in all of these cases. Where the businessman set aside time for search, this activity seemed to be more effective.

## "Gresham's Law" of planning

The third and final hypothesis that we shall consider states, "When an individual is faced both with highly

[6] March and Simon, p. 116, have constructed another model that deals with search for information more adequately. They did not intend that the general hypothesis describe behavior in the search for information.

[7] This is not a contradiction in the strict sense because of qualifications presented by March and Simon, p. 116.

programmed and highly unprogrammed tasks, the former tend to take precedence over the latter even in the absence of strong over-all time pressure."[8] This hypothesis is easiest to support empirically. In the dry cleaning case, routine tasks absorbed most of the decision maker's time, leaving little for searching out either information or alternatives. Both types of search were nonprogramed; both gave way to repetitive activities. The two wearing apparel cases also support the hypothesis.

In the coin laundry case, the wholesale liquor dealer case, the food products case, and others, time for search was planned beforehand. The result was more effective search activity. These decision makers devoted most of their time to nonprogramed (though planned) activity. If they felt that search was necessary, the time was available.

## EVALUATION AND PRESCRIPTION

*We submit* that search activity was performed quite ineffectively in the dry cleaning case and in the two wearing apparel cases. As a result, opportunity for profits was lost because profitable investments passed by unnoticed. On the other hand, search seemed more effective in the coin laundry and the wholesale liquor firm (also in the vending machine company and the billboard company described in the appendix). Sizable profits have resulted from the creative, imaginative, and aggressive search activity carried out in these firms.

These small businessmen who set aside time for search undoubtedly became more adept through practice and habit. They had time to search calmly for information when the occasion arose and to seek out attractive investment opportunities. They circumvented "Gresham's Law" of planning by allocating time for creative tasks.

If search is performed only at the times that dissatisfac-

[8] March and Simon, p. 185. ("Unprogrammed," as used here, is synonymous with "nonprogramed.")

tion sets in, it is likely that either routine work will not allow effective search or that time pressure will render the effort useless. Also, if search for alternatives takes place only when one becomes extremely dissatisfied, just one good alternative investment will be found at a time. When it is found, there will be no other proposals with which it can be compared, and therefore it must be evaluated on an absolute rather than a relative basis.

The successful searchers devote large portions of their time to building up a backlog of good investment proposals. When they decide to invest, the probability of choosing a profitable investment is increased by having this large reserve of possible investments. The most convincing case in point is that of the wholesale liquor dealer. He actually invested in a sales manager so that his own time would be available for search activity. Within three years, sales increased by about $1.5 million per year. Over this period, profits increased by over $200,000. Without search, this firm would have been quite marginal, but now it probably represents one of the most progressive and farsighted in the entire industry. The most important reasons for this phenomenal success are enough time to search for and investigate investment opportunities and an accumulation of pending projects with which new ideas could be compared.

It appears, then, that effective search need not be programed; perhaps it is even not amenable to programing. It is evident, however, that completely spontaneous search does not adequately accomplish its objective and that planning is required for the deliberate and creative search needed for difficult decisions.

If a businessman can choose from dozens of profitable investment proposals, he is less likely to select undesirable ventures. He can measure new proposals against a stockpile of opportunities. Aggressive search, by contributing to a backlog of investment proposals, can be the most constructive addition to the small businessman's kit of tools in the making of sound, profitable investment decisions.

*8*

# THE INVESTMENT DECISION-MAKING
# COMPLEX—A CASE STUDY

$\mathcal{T}HE$ $CASE$ studies covered up to this point have been concerned with one investment decision at a time and have frequently stressed only one aspect of the decision-making process. Investment decisions in actual business practice are much more complex, involving an overlapping sequence of diverse activity. There is no clear line between the time spent on other management activities and the time devoted to investment decisions. Within the maze of interrelated business activities, it is difficult to pick out the chain of events and decisions that leads to a particular investment.

This chapter presents an intensive case study of one

company, illustrating how investment proposals were conceived and analyzed; the information was obtained through sixteen interviewing sessions over a period of almost two years. The procedures uncovered were not optimal and could probably be improved, and some suggestions for improvement are discussed later.

## THE RYNDALL TIRE COMPANY

*The Ryndall* Tire Company is engaged in the sale of new tires and the manufacture and sale of recapped tires. It was founded in 1951 by Jack Ryndall, who is the president and general manager. From 1951 to 1955 annual sales mushroomed from $3,000 to about $210,000. During this period, expectations were high and facilities were expanded. Sales and profits reached a peak in 1956, then fell in the recession of 1957-58. Originally housed in a rented garage, the firm, after two years, purchased a larger building and erected an addition. Then, as further expansion seemed inevitable, the company purchased two adjacent, low-class apartment buildings for the eventual expansion of recapping and sales facilities. In the meantime (from 1956 to 1959) the company leased the apartments to low income families. In these four years, net income from the two apartment buildings averaged about $2,500 per year, a minor portion of the company's annual profits of $20,000 to $30,000.

From the beginning, the Ryndall Tire Company produced the best tires, using only the highest quality rubber available. Mr. Ryndall believed that a high-quality product, although more costly, was the keystone to business success; the company has never deviated from this policy.

Retail sales accounted for only 25 percent of the firm's volume. Since they carried a 20 percent higher markup than wholesale sales, the president wanted to increase retail volume. Accordingly, in 1957 a direct mail advertising campaign, lasting four months and costing over $1,000, was conducted through a local advertising agency; however, it proved unsuccessful. Neither the service manager nor Mr. Ryndall remembered getting any new retail customers as a result.

*Organization*

Jack Ryndall, president and general manager, personally decided all questions of consequence. Under the general manager were two executive salesmen who were minority stockholders and received a salary plus commissions. Occasionally, the salesmen made pricing decisions, but usually Mr. Ryndall was consulted. Previous to the interviews, a service manager was also employed to handle the installation and sales of tires at the plant. He supervised the recapping plant and inspected trade-in tires. In addition, the company employed three men in the recapping department and two to four men for tire changes and minor repairs.

*The president's state of mind in the summer of 1959*

By the summer of 1959, Mr. Ryndall's feelings about the future were mixed. On the one hand, he was optimistic about the remainder of 1959. On the other, he was somewhat worried about the future. He could rationalize the poor showing in 1958 because of the recession, but why was there no sales resiliency in 1957 and the first half of 1959? And what would 1960 and the years to follow hold in store?

He was determined to build sales and profits. His head buzzed with ideas, but he had little time to think them through. Seventy-five percent of the company's revenue depended upon wholesale sales to fleet owners. Since fleet owners were extremely price conscious, a tough competitive battle was usual in that market. Mr. Ryndall believed that these sales were a result of hard, aggressive selling and that any letup on determined effort meant lost sales and reduced profits. Consequently, he was torn between devoting his time to immediate sales or giving more attention to longer run prospects. If he devoted his time to selling tires, additional profits were assured, whereas the profits in analyzing prospective ventures were quite uncertain. In practice, he devoted his time to both sales and routine activities, neglecting the analysis of investment projects.

*Three investment proposals*

In the summer of 1959, three possible proposals faced Mr. Ryndall. The first involved a tire dealer in a small rural town who wanted Mr. Ryndall to organize a recapping plant and then spend two or three days each month resolving any problems that might arise. The tire dealer came to Mr. Ryndall with this proposition, but offered no specific salary.

The second proposal was suggested by a salesman selling new tire molds. At this time the Ryndall Tire Company owned eight horizontal steam-heated molds which occupied the entire floor space in the recapping plant. The proposed vertical molds were electrically heated and, although little was known about the difference in variable costs, required about half as much floor space. Therefore, the vertical molds could double the existing recapping capacity at a cost of $10,000. In Mr. Ryndall's mind, the new molds represented progress and modernization, a prerequisite for success in recapping. This attitude was expressed by his statement, "You have to say ahead in this business or you fall way behind." He thought that the old molds could be sold for $7,000 or $8,000. Cost savings seemed unimportant in this possible purchase. "If there are cost savings, I doubt that they would be sizable, but a higher quality tire might be possible with the new molds." The whole question of new equipment hinged largely on the small-town tire dealer. If he were willing to purchase the old molds for $7,000 or $8,000, Mr. Ryndall could purchase new molds. If not, it was unlikely that the old molds would sell for $7,000.

The third possibility concerned establishing a branch retail store in another part of town. Mr. Ryndall thought the location of his plant contributed to the failure of the

110

1957 advertising compaign. Because of one-way streets and heavy industrial traffic, the plant's location was relatively inaccessible. A branch retail store in a better location might stimulate retail tire sales and permit sales of automobile accessories.

None of these three ideas was carefully analyzed. Mr. Ryndall's evaluations were almost completely nonquantitative and subjective in nature and were made at lunch or in his spare time at home. He occasionally discussed these opportunities with the two salesmen and one or two business associates.

*The decision-making process*

The three alternatives were considered simultaneously, sometimes attention concentrating on one and then on another, without any plan. Only a hospital confinement provided Mr. Ryndall with time to reflect on the total situation. While undergoing a minor operation, he questioned his policy on high quality. Over a period of years the low-priced, low-quality competitors had attracted many former wholesale customers. This seemed to be the only time during the interview period that any doubt crept into his mind concerning quality. At this time, Mr. Ryndall was extremely pessimistic about the future of his firm. After leaving the hospital, he reconsidered the three alternatives.

1. Because he was working so hard, he did not have enough time to organize the other recapping plant; his services at his own plant seemed too valuable.

2. The decision on the first alternative precluded the possibility of selling the tire molds to the other dealer. Mr. Ryndall then discovered that the eight old molds would bring no more than $3,000. He also learned that the automobile manufacturers had designed smaller tires for the compact cars. The new vertical molds would not help him adapt his plant to the shift in demand for smaller tires. On the basis of these facts, he decided against the purchase of new equipment for at least two to five years.

111

3. In July of 1959 Mr. Ryndall began again to give attention to the proposal of the branch retail store. The future of the branch store was discussed in a meeting. Mr. Ryndall decided to examine some possible retail locations. A trade association suggested that not more than 5 percent of gross sales should be spent for rent. This rule of thumb suggested a location renting for about $200 per month. The basis for this figure is not clear; apparently at this stage $48,000 was the estimated annual sales of the branch store. A salesman was assigned the task of checking a few listings in the newspaper within this rental range. One of the salesmen could manage the branch store, and one or two of the lot men and a truck could be transferred to the branch. A total investment of $2,000 was estimated for necessary extra equipment. Recapping would continue in the existing plant and the tires trucked to the retail location whenever necessary. Since the new tires were granted on consignment, an increase in working capital seemed unnecessary.

Later in July the salesman and Mr. Ryndall looked at one location, a service station on a heavily traveled main street of the city. The rent was $400 per month. At this point, for several possible reasons, search bogged down. In 1958 the service manager was discharged, making it necessary for Mr. Ryndall or one of the two salesmen to remain at the plant. Realizing the importance of each of the two salesmen, Mr. Ryndall felt that neither could possibly be spared; the establishment of a retail store would require the full-time services of one. Undoubtedly, this was an important reason for the slowdown of search. An unsatisfactory rental agreement was probably another factor. In addition, by the fall of 1959, business was good, and with an increased workload for the salesmen and satisfactory sales, the branch store idea was slowly dying.

## A new alternative in 1960

The Ryndall Tire Company had previously purchased

two apartment buildings for future plant expansion. The apartments were being rented until extra plant capacity was needed. This need never materialized. Early in 1960, Mr. Ryndall was informed that a third apartment building on his block was for sale. The owner, who had also owned the other two, quoted a price of $14,000.

During the next few months, when time permitted, the president thought more about this apartment building. It was rumored that urban renewal might include his block; if this developed, the firm would profit. Also, if the third building were purchased, the firm would own the entire side of one block. Mr. Ryndall speculated that if a large company required this much land, the purchase of another building would place the Ryndall Tire Company in a good bargaining position.

In another meeting with the salesmen and a business associate he concluded that if the apartments continued at three-quarters occupancy, the building would pay for itself in five years (at a cost of $10,000). "If real estate pays for itself in ten years, it is a fair buy and this would take only five." Mr. Ryndall emphasized the fact that rental property required very little of his time. In the summer of 1960 the company offered $9,500 for the apartment building, but this amount was not acceptable to the owner. By this time two other developments were in progress.

1. In a trade association meeting with other small recappers the idea of educational advertising occurred to Ryndall. If the public knew more about the quality and price advantages of recapped tires—he reasoned—there would be less consumer resistance. Increasing acceptability of the tires would be advantageous to all small recappers.

At this time, sales had resumed a high level and Mr. Ryndall was now optimistic. Increased sales were probably responsible for a change in his thinking. Earlier he believed that his plant was relatively inaccessible to retail consumers. By the summer of 1960, he thought that another advertising program might bring retail sales to a more satisfactory level.

113

2. He sought a line of tires for foreign automobiles because the firm had received requests for them. After several contracts, a high-quality, high-priced line was stocked.

In August, 1960, the firm purchased the third apartment building for $11,500. Ryndall stated that the firm would buy more buildings in the future. There were many reasons. The return from rental property was adequate for the effort required. Perhaps more important was the uncertainty about the future of the tire business. Although sales were satisfactory at the time, Mr. Ryndall had just witnessed the first recession in his business since its founding. Diversification, which was at the time being praised by a trade association, might alleviate part of the risk in the future. Mr. Ryndall was also convinced that the firm would not undergo the tremendous growth that he had once envisioned, but he was not content to settle for the reduced position. His income was still much beneath the personal goals that he had fashioned.

## EVALUATION

*The Ryndall* Tire Company seems successful; it is doubtful that managerial goals would be better accomplished by a revision of its investment procedures. Nevertheless, it seems worthwhile to discuss the ways in which decision-making procedures in this and many other firms could be improved.

### Rationing of managerial time

Like any other scarce resource, a manager's time should be rationed according to its earning power. This is more easily said than done, but it is clear from our interviews that small businessmen give far too little attention to the allocation of their time. Not only is this resource precious, but it is irretrievable. Although quantification of its value is either difficult or impossible, some evaluation should be made, a task which involves taking stock of the areas that consume a manager's time and the jobs which should be performed, but are not.

114

To illustrate how this evaluation might be accomplished, we return to the case of Jack Ryndall. He uses about 50 percent of his time for sales and sales-connected work, such as pricing and promotion. Forty percent goes into performance of routine tasks such as technical supervision of the recapping plant, inspection of tires, and supervising tire changes. The remaining 10 percent is consumed in search and planning activities. Two neglected areas of investment management stand out: (a) search for available investment opportunities and (b) analysis of investment proposals. Better planning might provide more time for these functions. The supervision of the recapping plant and the inspection of trade-in tires could possibly be delegated to other personnel. Many sales result from retail customers coming to the plant; these sales could be handled by someone else. If the existing staff is incapable of taking on additional duties, one solution is to hire another man.

Formal planning of the expenditure of managerial time is not as important as the realization that opportunity costs are connected with the use of this resource. The best apportionment could be approximated by trial and error. If time is made available, a small businessman can take a broad perspective and view the firm as a whole. He can ask himself, "Where is the firm headed and why?" After goals have been determined, the manager can search for ways to further the firm's objectives. He might search for problem areas or examine apparent deficiencies in the operation of the company.

The case of Jack Ryndall exemplifies this point. He might spend more time reading trade publications. Although he does browse through some publications, he lets many ideas pass by unnoticed each month. Such ideas include technological improvements, new selling techniques, and improvement of internal management. For example, one trade publication described how a recapper boosted his sales of recapped tires by wrapping them in clear cellophane and making them appear comparable to new tires. He could

115

devote more attention to the rearrangement and analysis of his financial statements. He believes that recapped tires are more profitable than new tires; his financial statements show that the gross profit is about 27 percent for recaps and 16-20 percent for new tires. But a rearrangement of some of the other costs suggests that the contribution to overhead and profits is as high on new tires as on recaps. Furthermore, the profit margin on premium tires is lower than that on standard tires; if the margin on the premium lines becomes any lower, higher profits would result from pushing the standard tires. Finally, he could devote more time to developing the ideas which do come to him but which he does not now analyze adequately.

Mr. Ryndall does not find the time to analyze his proposals thoroughly; this was especially true of the retail store, on which he possessed some subjective notion about profitability. A more precise study would be revealing. In order to suggest one method by which Mr. Ryndall might have approached this problem, the interviewer prepared a profit study of the proposed branch store.

*Profit study of the branch store*

On the basis of past sales, gross profit was 26 percent on recaps, 17 percent on new tires, and 25 percent on used tires. If retail sales carried an extra 20 percent markup, then gross profit on tires would be roughly as follows: 46 percent on recaps, 37 percent on new tires, and 45 percent on used tires. Mr. Ryndall estimated that a retail store should sell about 60 percent new tires, 30 percent recaps, and 10 percent used tires. A 40 percent gross profit on sales results from such a product mix.

One implicit estimate of annual sales for the retail store was $48,000. However, when Mr. Ryndall was asked to make probability-level guesses of annual sales, he answered as follows: "It is almost a sure thing to do $70,000. This is probably the lowest. Chances of doing $80,000 are about 60 percent—of doing $90,000 are about 55 percent. There is about a 50 percent chance for $100,000 and little chance of doing much over that."[1]

Next, it is necessary to estimate the incremental costs of the new branch. Two extra men would eventually be required for tire changes and other miscellaneous jobs ($5,500 per year). If one of the salesmen was moved to the branch store, a new salesman would be hired to replace him ($5,000). There would be other expenses—rent $3,000; utilities $850; insurance $200; part-time bookkeeper $1,200; extra commissions, 5 percent of sales; professional fees $100; and added depreciation $200. Figure 8-1 and Table 8-1 summarize this information.

TABLE 8-1

INCREMENTAL PROFIT ESTIMATES, RYNDALL TIRE COMPANY, 1959

| Annual sales volume | $48,000 | $70,000 | $80,000 | $90,000 | $100,000 | $110,000 |
|---|---|---|---|---|---|---|
| Gross profit (40%) | 19,200 | 28,000 | 32,000 | 36,000 | 40,000 | 44,000 |
| Other (fixed) expenses | 16,050 | 16,050 | 16,050 | 16,050 | 16,050 | 16,050 |
| Commissions | 2,400 | 3,500 | 4,000 | 4,500 | 5,000 | 5,500 |
| Net profit (40% GP) | 750 | 8,450 | 11,950 | 15,450 | 18,950 | 22,450 |

Figure 8-1 shows that the break-even point is about $45,000 annual sales at a 40 percent average markup. To hedge the investment somewhat, in the beginning, no new men would be required. By using one employee from the present plant instead of hiring two new employees, $5,500 would be saved annually. This brings the break-even point down to about $30,000. If and when the store operated at a satisfactory sales level, one or two employees (when required) could be hired.

Probably the total investment would be somewhat

[1] It appears that either Mr. Ryndall had become more optimistic about the possibilities of a retail store or he made a mistake somewhere, because the $70,000 floor on sales in a branch store is considerably more than the $48,000 figure assumed a year earlier. Nevertheless, both assumptions are considered.

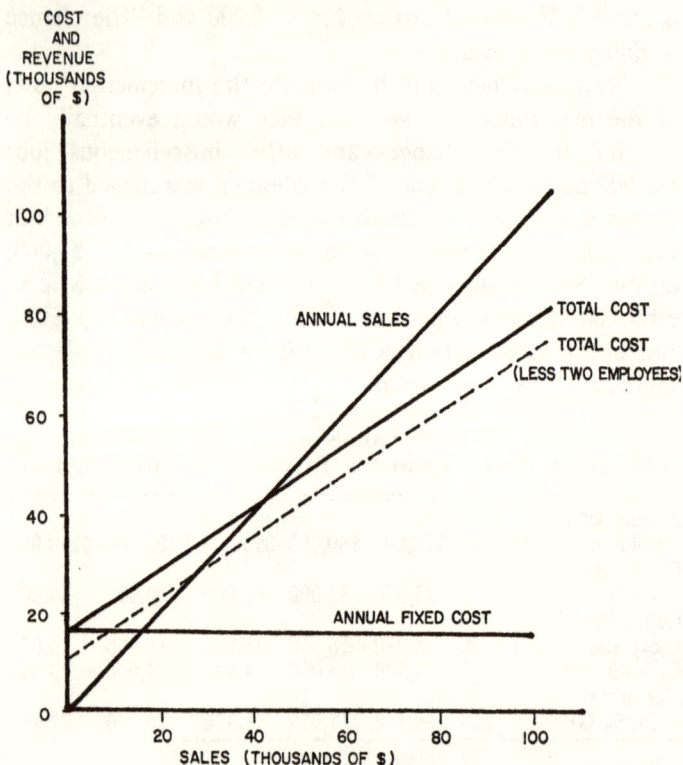

FIGURE 8-1

BREAK-EVEN CHART FOR PROPOSED RETAIL STORE,
RYNDALL TIRE COMPANY

more than $2,000. Working capital for accounts receivable
and initial promotional expenditure might require another
$1,000 to $2,000. The total investment of $3,000 to $4,000
would be paid back in less than a year even at the pessimistic
sales estimate of $70,000. This analysis indicates that the
investment would be extremely profitable. It should be
reemphasized that this evaluation of the branch store was
performed by the interviewer and not by a company official.

If this same study were undertaken using only the
allocations and other information taken directly from the

financial statements, the branch store would appear to be unprofitable. But if incremental reasoning is used—only considering additional revenues and costs that result from the decision—the store appears to be a profitable venture. The interviews failed to reveal with certainty whether Mr. Ryndall was thinking incrementally when he subjectively analyzed the proposal. If he were not, the explanation of his failure to invest is simple. His cost estimates, however, seem to indicate that he was, in general, thinking in terms of revenue and cost increments. Investment analysis, like other economic analysis, is not usually meaningful in any other framework. If small businessmen do not use incremental reasoning in their analysis for investments, then perhaps their first need is for a reorientation in thinking.

The Ryndall Tire Company provides an excellent illustration of routine activity driving out more creative tasks and of the pressure of time forcing hasty decisions. The case suggests that small businessmen might profit heavily simply from finding some systematic method of outlining the alternatives and consequences involved in making different decisions. Decision making in actual practice is difficult, partly because of the complex interrelations among real life problems. With such confusion, some systematic approach appears essential. Devices such as break-even charts or payoff tables can be useful because they force the manager to think in a comparatively organized way about the consequences connected with a particular act. In organizing analysis, they thereby save precious time for further creativity.

*9*

## CONCLUSION

$\mathcal{J}$ HUS FAR comments on two of the functions of capital budgeting, forecasting the supply and cost of capital and postauditing, are conspicuously absent from the discussion. The previous chapters have neglected the supply and cost of capital for several reasons. First, the subject is relatively undeveloped. Although a great deal of literature on the cost of capital exists, most of it is highly theoretical; there is little that is of practical value to the small businessman. John Lintner has published an excellent article that reviews most of the important developments in this area.[1] Second, the problem of budgeting funds for investment purposes does not yet appear to be a major problem in the firms that we have studied. Apparently the budgeting of funds does not become necessary until a stockpile of investment proposals causes an excess demand for the firm's investment funds. These stockpiles rarely exist in our cases because the managers place insufficient stress on finding or following up investment possibilities. Thus, improved procedures for discovering investment opportunities should take priority over measurements of cost and availability of capital. This comment does not imply that the forecasting of funds and their cost is unimportant in capital budgeting, but that in most cases, small businessmen have not yet advanced to the state that these forecasts would benefit them.

The postauditing function is also neglected in our discussion. The small businessman subjectively evaluates past investments every time he estimates costs or revenues for a new investment proposal. With a small volume of investment decisions formal postaudits may not be needed to improve management's forecasting or estimating ability. In large firms the formal postaudit is a device for control of subordinates; since most of the businessmen in our study make all the investment decisions themselves, this control feature is unnecessary. As the organization of a firm expands and the volume of investments undertaken increases, the postaudit function grows in importance.

With regard to formulas for ranking investment proposals, this study has resulted in two conclusions.

1. We find that when future costs and revenues are relatively certain, simpler formulas to rank investments in order of profitability (such as rate of income on investment and the MAPI rate of return[2]) often place investment proposals in about the same order as the more complicated

[1] John Lintner, "Dividends, Earnings, Leverage, Stock Prices, and the Supply of Capital to Corporations," *Review of Economics and Statistics*, XLIV (August 1960), 243-69.

[2] The MAPI rate of return is complicated and refined with respect to its derivation but quite simple to use.

measures. When we recognize the existence of uncertainty in revenue and cost estimates, there is a strong case for deemphasis of esoteric measures and substitution of simpler methods. This deemphasis is especially applicable to small businessmen not acquainted with theoretical formulas. Under conditions of certainty (and perfect competition) present value is unquestionably the most rational approach to the evaluation of prospective investments. The present value formula, however, assumes that all future costs and revenues are known, that the opportunity cost on all other investments is also known and invariant throughout time, and that the time period of comparison is the same for all proposals being considered. But even if actual investment proposals are ranked according to present value, uncertainty may destroy the significance of the ranking. In the real world, the payback period, used with caution, may be an entirely satisfactory criterion for choice.

2. Instead of stressing refinement in ranking methods, many small businessmen can more profitably improve their capital budgeting procedures by setting aside a portion of the manager's or owner's time: time to view the firm as a whole and evaluate its progress; time to correct weak policies and practices and to emphasize those that are strong; time to search for and stockpile alternative prospective investments and information concerning them; time to assess the availability of funds; and time to compare and choose among alternatives. The extent to which each of these tasks adds to a firm's profits will vary widely among companies, but most important is making time available. For if it is not reserved, then routine tasks tend to dominate, while more creative and demanding jobs are left undone.

Earlier chapters supported these conclusions with empirical evidence from investment decisions concerning expansion and innovation. Rather than repeat the earlier discussion, we present new case material on replacement investments, indicating that the main conclusions of this study also apply in that sphere.

*The replacement* of trucks would appear to be a problem suited to such refined treatment as present value analysis. Truck replacements involve a minimum of uncertainty and a maximum of information. Here, if anywhere, one might reason, small firms would benefit from current developments in capital budgeting. This section reviews several cases to test the validity of this proposition, starting with a truck leasing firm.

## XYZ *Truck Leasing Company*

The xyz Company possessed 31 trucks of various sizes. Mileage and cost data were maintained for each truck. But these records were not used for replacement purposes. The owner stated that he replaced trucks when they accumulated about 100,000 miles. Upon investigation, however, it was found that his previous trucks had been driven only 50,000 or 60,000 miles. When reexamined on this point, the owner admitted that the 100,000 mile policy was never given serious thought and that the trucks had been replaced for other reasons such as impending overhauls, undercapacity, improved technology, and accidents.

It first appeared that the cost data would permit a meaningful determination of optimum truck life. But this was not the case. The cost figures for individual trucks followed no meaningful pattern, and since they contained little predictive value, expensive, refined replacement analysis would have been meaningless. The data were subject to two serious limitations: they covered a short mileage span and they included information on only two or three trucks of the same make and model.

Another study[3] analyzed optimal replacement policy for truck-tractor power units under more auspicious conditions.

[3] Vernon L. Smith, "Economic Equipment Policies: An Evaluation," *Management Science*, IV (October 1957), 20-37. Reprinted in Edward H. Bowman and Robert B. Fetter (eds.), *Analyses of Industrial Operations* (Homewood, Ill.: Richard D. Irwin, 1959), pp. 444-62.

A careful statistical study of a large trucking firm that purchased 240 power units of the same make, model, and year showed that relatively small costs were incurred by delaying the purchase of new trucks past the optimum life. The conclusion was that actual practice and optimum replacement policy are not likely to differ greatly.

Smith's analysis required a great deal of time and would ordinarily have cost thousands of dollars. In short, such research would not be worth its cost to a trucking firm, especially to one with a diversity of trucks. Another, less sophisticated study[4] concluded that trucks between about three and ten years of age have similar average annual operating costs and from this standpoint it made the difference when they were replaced.

## IMPLICATIONS OF THE STUDIES

*Refined* replacement analysis is both difficult and expensive and may not result in sufficient savings to justify the cost of research. If large firms with vast financial resources, specialized labor, and ideal research conditions cannot profit from the use of refinement in replacement analysis, then neither can the small trucker or truck leasing firm.

How then, can the owner of the xyz truck leasing firm use his time more effectively? As suggested earlier in this chapter, he can set aside time for search activity. For example the xyz Company's trucks are repaired at a local garage instead of on its own premises. When questioned about this practice, the owner explained that when he started the business with three trucks, this seemed the most reasonable policy; as the firm grew, he never reevaluated the maintenance procedures. A study analyzing the cost of maintenance by the garage and comparing it with the cost of self-maintenance by a company mechanic might reveal significant savings. The present maintenance plan may still

[4] Howard Willett, "How Long Should You Run a Truck Before You Replace It?" *Fleet Owner*, XXII (September 1953), 62-65.

be best; but if expansion continues, the day will come when self-performance of maintenance should be considerably cheaper. Search activity can reveal the time for policy change and the magnitude of possible savings.

Much of the current literature suggests that refinement of technique is the solution to investment problems, a contention for which there seems to be no empirical evidence. The alternative investments open to the businessman and the information concerning each are often assumed to be known. The main theme of this volume is that this information is not known; and because of great amounts of uncertainty and partial information, small businessmen should not worry greatly about their failure to use refined analyses but should be more concerned with discovering new opportunities and collecting better information. The real need in small business investments is for greater imagination and creativity.

# CONTINUOUS VERSUS DISCRETE DISCOUNTING

$\mathcal{T}$HE METHOD of discounting presented in Chapter 3 assumes that the entire amount of income or saving is produced at the very end of each year. In actual practice returns are spread out over a year. To be more precise[1]

$$V = \int_0^n Q(t)e^{-rt}\, dt + Se^{-rn} - C$$

where $V$ = present value in excess of acquisition cost,

$\quad Q(t)$ = the continuous equation for income or saving over time,

$\quad C$ = acquisition cost of the asset,

$\quad e$ = 2.71828, the base of natural logarithms,

$\quad n$ = the time period in which the asset is sold or discarded,

$\quad r$ = the discounting rate of interest,

$\quad t$ = time,

$\quad S$ = salvage value at year $n$.

In most cases this formulation unnecessarily complicates the analysis. Normally, there is little difference between the continuous and discontinuous formulations.[2] For example, by using the above continuous formula, $100 due at the end of ten years at 10 percent interest is worth $36.79 today and by using the discrete formula presented in Chapter 3, it is worth $38.55 today. For most practical purposes, the error due to uncertainty amounts to much more than this. As the interest rate and the length of the asset's life increase, the error committed by discrete discounting also increases. For 25 years at 20 percent interest the difference is about 57 percent of the largest figure, but for five years at 5 percent interest the difference is less than one percent.

[1] Edward H. Bowman and Robert B. Fetter, *Analysis for Production Management* (Homewood, Ill.: Richard D. Irwin, 1957), p. 315.
[2] Solomon, *Management of Corporate Capital*, p. 321.

# THE INFINITE CHAIN

$\mathcal{T}HE$ LUTZES[1] differentiate between different types of "horizons." If an entrepreneur buys a machine and never replaces it, his horizon is called a single machine horizon. If the machine is bought and replaced at some future date, and the replacement is replaced at some future date, *ad infinitum*, then this is called an infinite horizon (infinite chain of machines). The entrepreneur's horizon extends indefinitely into the future, during which time there is a chain of machines, one being discarded and the next being its replacement. The discrete form of excess present value over cost for the infinite chain of machines is

$$V = \left[ \frac{Q_1}{(1+r)} + \frac{Q_2}{(1+r)^2} + \cdots + \frac{Q_n + S}{(1+r)^n} - C \right]$$

$$\times \left[ 1 + \frac{1}{(1+r)^n} + \frac{1}{(1+r)^{2n}} + \cdots \right]$$

$$= \left[ \frac{Q_1}{(1+r)} + \frac{Q_2}{(1+r)^2} + \cdots + \frac{Q_n + S}{(1+r)^n} - C \right]$$

$$\times \frac{(1+r)^n}{(1+r)^n - 1} \tag{4}$$

where $V$ = excess present value over cost,
$\quad Q_t$ = annual cash flows,
$\quad S$ = salvage value,
$\quad r$ = rate of interest,
$\quad n$ = life of asset,
$\quad C$ = cost of asset.

Equation (4) assumes that the earnings and the life of each asset in the chain are identical. The difference between equation (1) in Chapter 3 and equation (4) is *not* slight. To exemplify this difference, suppose that the following cash flows and salvage values of a proposal are forthcoming.

| Year | Cash inflow (saving) | Salvage value |
|---|---|---|
| 1 | $2,000 | $6,000 |
| 2 | 1,900 | 5,500 |
| 3 | 1,800 | 5,000 |
| 4 | 1,700 | 4,000 |
| 5 | 1,600 | 3,800 |
| 6 | 1,500 | 3,600 |
| 7 | 1,400 | 3,400 |
| 8 | 1,300 | 3,200 |
| 9 | 1,200 | 3,000 |
| 10 | 1,100 | 2,800 |

10 percent discounting rate of interest
Acquisition cost of asset = $8,000

Using the infinite chain of machines formula (4), we find the excess present value to be $5,012. Using the single machine formula (1), we find the excess present value to be $3,080. Formula (4) tells us that this asset will pay for itself and *all future replacements*, yield a 10 percent return (over and above paying for the asset) *forever* and also yield an excess present value of $5,012. Formula (1) tells us that the asset will pay for itself, yield a 10 percent return, and

[1] Lutz, p. 107.

129

have an excess present value of $3,080 *for just ten years.* Formula (4) assumes a status quo to eternity; the earnings of all future machines (or assets) will be the same. In the fluid commercial atmosphere of today, this assumption is improbable. Uncertainty is the ever-present, never-yielding foe of the businessman. Asking him to forecast until doomsday is an unreasonable request. Probably the machine that replaces the existing facility will have a different earnings schedule and a different acquisition cost.

The difference between the two formulations may, on the other hand, be less profound than is apparent. If a decision maker always uses the infinite chain formula, the present value of proposals will be larger than if he always uses the single machine formula. In either case, however, the relevant figure is the relationship between specific proposals. Perhaps the infinite chain formula serves to raise aspiration levels in a superficial way; but over a period of time both formulas may lead to about the same investments. The infinite chain formula does eliminate the problem of unequal comparison periods of two investment proposals and in this way serves a useful function. More empirical research is required on this topic before we can determine which formulation is better suited to which types of investment problems.

  $S$ = salvage value,

  $n$ = life of asset,

 $C$ = cost of asset.

# CASE STUDIES

## DRY CLEANER CASE

$\mathcal{J}$N THIS case the owner had very few alternative investment opportunities with which he could compare the proposal described below. We feel that additional search for
alternatives and information would have been helpful.

HISTORY

Mr. E owned a small dry cleaning plant which he had
inherited many years ago. During the war he had accumulated
a sizable sum of money, most of which was invested in stocks,
ranging from blue chip to highly speculative issues; most of the
stocks are now double or triple their original cost. More recently,
Mr. E, with the aim of diversifying his holdings, has been
investing in mutual funds. Mr. E feels that his firm should
stand on its own feet; hence he has not invested his extra
personal funds in the business. His investments in stocks come
from his personal funds; no assets of the firm are invested in
stocks.

Mr. E is not highly enthusiastic about the future of his
business. He thinks that if a dry cleaner is to survive today, he
must work hard to expand sales. The market is not growing and
the per capita sales are falling. Therefore, only the most aggressive firms will survive.

BRANCH STORE

The promoter of a new shopping center offered Mr. E space

in it. He told Mr. E that the surrounding area consisted of a growing suburbia and gave data concerning the population and the income of the inhabitants.

After talking to a banker and another business associate and after having viewed the site of the shopping center, Mr. E computed a break-even point. Using the figures we have cited in a previous chapter, he decided that even the most conservative estimates would allow him a profit; so he invested.

## WEARING APPAREL MANUFACTURER A

*This firm* analyzed one proposal at a time, seemingly without much concern for the relative merits of other investments. We believe that further search might have greatly benefited this company.

### POLICY

Mr. F, president of the firm, stated that the first year's revenue from prospective investments must equal the cost of the investment before the company is willing to invest. This policy would suggest a backlog of potentially profitable investments and a shortage of capital. But further investigation revealed a surplus of cash, many short term securities, and an unused line of bank credit.

### MERGER

A yard goods mill in financial difficulty was offered to Mr. F. After a quick look at the financial statements of the distressed firm, it was decided that since the investment would not be returned in one year, the deal would be forgotten. This proposal was apparently not compared with any other investment.

### MACHINERY

An equipment salesman brought a new label printing machine to the attention of Mr. F. The company had been purchasing labels, and the new machine offered a great deal of potential savings. Since the estimated savings for one year were greater than the price of the machine, it was purchased.

### SALES

This firm was emphatically sales-minded, perhaps to the exclusion of other aspects of the business. This emphasis has evidently proved satisfactory; therefore, no reason to change the managerial goals seems to exist.

New building

At one time this firm rented space in a small multifloor building. As the company grew, the building became more and more unsuitable. Mr. F. decided that a new building was necessary to keep costs in line with competition and to provide room for extra capacity. Search was undertaken for a building that could be rented. The search proved fruitless and a new building was decided upon. The one-year payback criterion was not used here. In fact, no estimates of savings were calculated.

## WEARING APPAREL MANUFACTURER B

*This case* illustrates the management of a firm in which investment decisions are evidently unimportant. The management seems to have no backlog of possible investment opportunities and seldom finds a need to evaluate investment proposals.

Organization

The firm employs about 50 people. Two partners are the principal owners. Mr. G is the president, general manager, and owner of majority interest in the company. He makes the final decision concerning all capital investments.

C' y attitudes

G stated that occasionally an investment proposal is considered, but it is usually quite minor in terms of the required capital. For example, within the previous six months a salesman suggested a switch to electric typewriters. A saving would result from improved secretarial morale and reduced fatigue. The largest saving would come from an attachment that simulates spirit masters. Spirit masters are the present invoice medium and are run off in several copies after typing.

Mr. G said that these attachments would save their cost in one year, because a light weight paper could be used instead of the regular spirit masters.

This investment was obviously an extremely profitable one. Had there been a smaller savings, the evaluation of the proposal would have become more difficult. Interviews with Mr. G seemed to indicate that under these circumstances the typewriters would not have been bought, since analysis of such problems is generally not undertaken. The information on cost savings was given to the firm by a salesman and no search was undertaken.

Mr. G. stated that retaining present customers and gaining new ones is the primary problem of the company. "If extra effort is to be expended, it will probably be in this field." Technological change is not so rapid that any serious difficulty arises by neglecting most new capital developments.

# AUTOMATIC COIN LAUNDRY CASE

*In this* case determined search effort is an extremely important part of the decision-making process. We conclude on a subjective basis that the search was profitable and worth the time spent.

HISTORY

For many years Mr. X, a rather successful businessman, has made diverse investments—from securities to apartment buildings. He claims that he is always looking for a good investment. "My minimum requirement is that the cash or short-term capital invested is returned in three to three and one-half years." From the interviews with Mr. X, it is apparent that investment opportunities of this nature do not frequently appear. When asked why he uses this three to three and one-half year criterion, he stated that it generally produced profitable investments. He mentioned that this criterion was not used in connection with stocks and bonds, only on tangible investments.

STIMULUS

Late in 1959, Mr. X had accumulated a cash balance and decided that instead of investing in a savings and loan association at 4 to 5 percent interest, he would look for a better investment. He made two stipulations: the proposal should involve about $6,000 cash, and it should require a minimum of supervision on Mr. X's part.

ALTERNATIVE PROPOSALS

During this period, he contemplated at least three possible proposals. (1) He considered establishing a stock investment company; however, this would require a great deal of supervision and more cash than he was willing to invest ($15,000 or more). He did not reject the idea, but decided to direct his immediate attention to other possibilities.

(2) He considered investing in rental real estate, but he concluded that most of the cash received in the form of rent payments would go for mortgage payments. Rental property

met two of his criteria (no supervision and small cash outlay), but it would not return his cash in three to three and one-half years. So he rejected this idea. The rejection of these proposals was not instantaneous. The conclusions concerning them were formulated over a period of a month or two. During this time, Mr. X was looking for something "better."

(3) A proposal, suggested by an advertisement in the newspaper, involved establishing an automatic coin-operated laundry. Upon contacting a washing machine sales representative, he found that the cash investment required was within his limits. This idea was quite appealing, because the time required for supervision would be limited.

## Location

A business associate was in the process of completing a building. Two or three people had already asked this associate about installing a coin-operated laundry in his new building, but the owner was hesitant. Extra sewer costs would be involved. When Mr. X talked to this associate, there was no controversy; if Mr. X desired, he could locate in the new building. Mr. X felt that the location was ideal, but he was uncertain about demand. He also had concluded that the equipment and fixtures would require about $15,000 cash plus a loan of about $25,000.

## Further search

In an effort to reduce the initial cash outlay, Mr. X contacted four or five different washer and dryer manufacturers. At this time he discovered there was little difference among manufacturers' prices. He also found that several manufacturers were willing to lend the necessary capital; they made strong recommendations that the laundry be composed of 50 washers and 20 dryers.

At this point, Mr. X had all of the problems solved except two: (a) the proposal involved more cash than he had anticipated, and (b) the investment's profitability was risky in light of the uncertainty of demand. Mr. X contacted an associate who had recently been searching for investment opportunities. The associate decided to invest if Mr. X felt that this coin-operated laundry was profitable. Mr. X and his associate began to search for information. They talked to factory representatives again. They visited four or five local prospective competitors, observing their methods of operation; they questioned housewives in these establishments concerning preferences and dissatisfactions connected with coin-operated laundries. They talked to owners in the surrounding area, and they engaged the

135

services of a manufacturer who sold a franchise "deal." Mr. X estimates that he spent more than 50 hours in this search.

## WHOLESALE LIQUOR DEALER CASE

*Here is* an example of extremely profitable search activity. It shows how a small businessman doubled sales volume and profits and clearly illustrates a case in which vigorous and purposive search can prove to be one of a firm's most important assets.

HISTORY

Immediately after World War II, Mr. D established a wholesale liquor company in a large town. He was and is one of the smallest wholesalers in that city. From 1946 to 1956 the firm's growth was slow. During most of this period Mr. D personally supervised all phases of operation—sales, finance, warehousing, delivery, purchasing, and office management. By 1956 he had delegated supervisory authority in all of these fields except finance and sales. The sales force had grown from four to six men, but Mr. D was very unhappy about his relatively slow growth rate. From 1950 to 1956, sales had climbed from $1 million to $1.5 million. Mr. D felt that a plateau had been reached because almost no increase had taken place during the 1954-1956 period. Between 1956 and 1959, sales increased to $3 million and profits increased proportionally.

ORGANIZATION

Most of Mr. D's time was consumed in sales supervision. Customers had complaints that required attention, salesmen had problems that couldn't wait, and as a result, sales promotion lagged behind competition. On top of this, Mr. D worked very long hours, which deprived him of time for family recreation and vacations. For years he felt that he could strengthen his business and cut costs if only the time were available. Finally, Mr. D found the best sales manager that he thought was available and offered him the highest salary that he had ever earned, and he accepted the job. Within three months he had assumed complete authority over the sales department.

Meanwhile, Mr. D decided to spend the majority of his time searching for cost-saving and sales-stimulating ideas. He maintained a file in which each new idea was recorded. The most important were examined first, and when further information was necessary, Mr. D had the time to perform the necessary research. This took the form of personal interviews with customers, talks with distillers, and visits to other wholesalers. From 1956 until 1960, literally hundreds of Mr. D's ideas were implemented.

## Wine sales and profits

Many of his plans were completely original. For example, Mr. D asked why wine sales had not been increasing. He was told by the salesmen and the sales manager that supermarkets wouldn't release more shelf space for their wine and, without larger display areas or promotional effort by the supermarkets, extra sales would not be possible unless the price were cut.

Wine margins are quite slim and many wholesalers in this country have discontinued selling wine in less than case lots because of the high marketing costs. Mr. D then stated that he would find a method to increase sales and profits of wine.

First, he talked with five or six supermarket managers and two supermarket chain executives. After these visits, he concluded that much could be done. Three ideas seemed to evolve from these meetings: wine was not properly displayed in supermarkets because of limited shelf space and lack of sufficient supermarket personnel; the bottles got dusty and looked unappetizing; the usual grocery pricing method left an otherwise beautiful label marred by a large black price. This practice also renders the wine unsuited for gifts because the price mark cannot be easily removed. Mr. D felt that if these disadvantages could be overcome, sales and profits would increase substantially.

The solution to this problem involved the purchase of a one and one-half ton van-type truck. Mr. D took one of his best employees out of the warehouse and gave him the title of wine supervisor. This man's function was to load his truck each morning with an ample stock of all wines, to visit (according to a preplanned schedule) a number of supermarkets, to dust previously stocked bottles, and to restock the shelves with merchandise, using a small gummed label to price each bottle of wine.

Mr. D had received permission from the executives of all chains to perform this service; they were more than happy to receive it, because Mr. D's wine supervisor saved the supermarket time and money by stocking and pricing merchandise. As a result, wine sales and profits increased by about 50 percent in six months. This was partially due to the fact that most supermarkets gave Mr. D a substantially increased amount of shelf space because of his valuable service.

137

An equipment salesman approached Mr. D with a report that showed Mr. D how much more efficient his organization could be if data processing equipment were installed. He also showed that Mr. D's profit picture could be improved considerably through the use of this equipment.

With the cost and revenue estimates before him, Mr. D carefully examined the benefits and costs that would be derived. He concluded that he possessed insufficient information to reach a decision, but one point was clear: when compared with other investment opportunities, the figures did not warrant the rental or the purchase of data processing equipment.

Mr. D was an imaginative manager with unusual vigor and ingenuity. The idea of possessing an information system intrigued him. He visited the establishments of several wholesale liquor dealers whose volume of business was comparable to his own volume; each was using a certain brand of data processing equipment. During these visits, he looked at financial records before and after installation. On the basis of this and on the subjective views of these businessmen, Mr. D decided not to invest in this type of equipment until his sales volume and the number of transactions had grown considerably larger.

### DIRECT TELEPHONES

Among Mr. D's many creative ideas was that of having a direct telephone line to a neighboring town. With this facility, retail liquor stores could telephone their orders and could be serviced much more rapidly than by a salesman. The previous company policy allowed any liquor retailer to call Mr. D's firm long distance collect, but retailers seemed to be reluctant to make these collect calls. Consequently, they waited for salesmen.

Mr. D made several trips to this town, talking to retailers and getting their views of the proposal. The installation of a "long line" was really part of a longer range plan in which "long lines" could be installed to dozens of towns in the state. Since the information received from talks with liquor retailers seemed to be inconclusive, he decided to experiment with only the one phone to record carefully all effects and to use the data to evaluate the long range plan. If this program proves successful, Mr. D may be able again to double sales and profits.

### MORE EFFICIENCY

At one time, salesmen used standard order pads. After an order was written, a secretary typed five copies. Obviously, this was unsatisfactory. Mr. D talked to associates and thought the problem through himself. After weeks of visits from equipment salesmen, Mr. D decided to invest in a duplicating machine. It involved a spirit process. Orders were written on spirit masters and then duplicated on the machine. One copy served as an invoice. This machine proved unsatisfactory for many reasons, one of which was the poor appearance of the invoices. After more search, Mr. D sold the spirit duplicator and purchased an automatic offset machine that cost about $1,400. This process produced impressive looking copies and was used for many other purposes, including a monthly bulletin to all of the salesmen.

## SALES MEETINGS

Mr. D felt also that the quality of sales meetings could be improved. Each new suggestion immediately went into a source file. After some time, the file contained numerous notions related to the subject. Some of them were the use of a tape recorder to play back the sales meeting to the salesmen, the use of an opaque projector to show salesmen brochures, advertisements, and other material, and the use of salesmen-directed meetings in which Mr. D and the sales manager were not present. Mr. D's theory on sales meetings consisted of using as many of the salesmen's sensory perceptions as possible, including taste.

## SALES CAMPAIGN

One particular brand of whisky was not being sold in adequate amounts to satisfy the distiller. If a wholesaler does not produce sufficient sales volume to satisfy the manufacturer, the franchise may be given to another wholesaler, a practice which is an ever-present problem for the wholesaler. Many sales campaigns had been attempted before, but all proved to be ineffective.

Mr. D planned his particular campaign to run for six months. The outstanding feature of it was emphasis on unusual appeals. With the help of the distiller, Mr. D conducted a contest among his salesmen. If a salesman sold 400 cases of this particular brand in a month, he received a new automobile. If he sold 40 cases, he received a high-fidelity phonograph. The salesmen were to appeal to each retail liquor dealer as a friend and not as an ordinary salesman. The salesmen told the liquor store owners that if each one sold one case of this particular brand in a month, the salesman could win a car. Since a great many customers enter a liquor store with no specific brand in mind, the retailer can sell large quantities of any brand he wishes to push. "If the retailer suggests something, there is a very good chance that the customer will purchase it." The campaign proved extremely successful.

# FOOD PRODUCTS COMPANY

*This case* illustrates a situation in which a creative search for alternatives (by top management) seems relatively unnecessary.

On the borderline between small and big business, this firm employs about 200 people. Every day investment proposals flow into the front office. So many of them come in that management has established rules for investment decisions.

The rule used is a payback criterion. If a proposal will pay for itself in one year or less, it is accepted, and if not, it is usually rejected. There are restrictions, however, on the amount of money involved.

While search for alternatives by management is almost nonexistent, search for information is integral. If a proposal looks promising but requires more than a year to pay back, it is studied further by some staff member. At times, a considerable amount of search effort is expended on a proposal, depending upon its immediate apparent profitability.

# BILLBOARD COMPANY

*The partners* of this firm seem to be constantly seeking new investment opportunities. Their search effort has been rewarding.

HISTORY

Two partners, who have made considerable profits in the billboard industry since World War II, are constantly interested in expanding their business and from time to time purchase other billboard companies.

POLICY AND ANALYSIS

From past experience the partners are quite familiar with the revenues and expenses connected with billboard operations. They also obtain income statements from the owners wishing to sell; they project these statements into the future to get an idea of the annual expected profits; and they take into account

140

additional revenues arising from changes in prices, wages, and salaries. They are greatly influenced by the price that they have most recently paid for billboards; if the current price has been around $300 per panel, the partners are reluctant to purchase billboards for more than this even though the investment appears profitable at the higher costs.

First year profit on projected income statement plays a primary role in their decision. The partners compute how long it will take to recover the funds invested (or to pay off money borrowed to finance the purchase), but they do not have clear ideas on a payback criterion. The partners take the quality of the panels into account, paying less for those requiring repair.

## Alternative investments

Since the partners are engaged in several lines of business, they are constantly aware of other investment opportunities. At times they make a careful comparison between profits on billboards and profits from alternate investment opportunities; judgment is made on an estimate of first year performance.

Sometimes a long period of negotiation is necessary to conclude the purchase. For example, they have been considering for more than a year the purchase of a company that owns rundown billboards. Since the advertising rates for this company are low, the partners will increase the rates and profitability of the firm if they purchase it. While they are certain that this operation would be profitable, they are not completely satisfied with the price asked by the owner. Apparently they believe that if they hold off, he may ask less.

## VENDING MACHINE COMPANY

*This case* illustrates how a backlog of profitable investment proposals can ease the problem of proposal evaluation.

## Policy

The vending machine company places machines in various types of establishments on a percentage basis, that is, a percentage of the receipts is usually given to a store owner who installs one of these vending machines.

Mr. H, the president of Vending Machine Enterprises, stated that he makes hundreds of investments each month. As he went through several different types of investments with the interviewer, it was evident that little, if any, quantitative analysis is performed on most of his projects.

Within the past year over 15 different types of new vending machines have been presented to Mr. H by salesmen. "Some have great potential, and others have very little." This is typical of Mr. H's quite subjective method of analysis. Mr. H constantly searches for new investment opportunities. The extent of his diversification is illustrated by such investments as purchase of other vending machine companies, purchase of Navy surplus paint, investment in potential oil-producing property, acquisition of a textile company in a foreign country, and construction of a large motel.

SEARCH

Mr. H finds more of these prospective investments than find him. He looks through foreign and domestic newspapers and searches within his vast network of business associates.

He stated, "There is no neat formula for making investments. You have to analyze each one with an eye to the future." He also stated that there are dozens of investments that are possible, but because of limited funds he can only skim off the best.

MERGER

Some of his investments have required a great deal of search for information. For example, one competitor offered to sell out to Mr. H. A group of five men—a lawyer, an accountant, two business associates, and Mr. H—spent almost a year of analysis before purchasing the company. The deal involved a considerable amount of money (nearly half a million dollars) and was the chief reason for so much analytical effort. This investment was unusual in this respect. Most of his decisions involve less capital and less quantification. They are usually more subjectively determined. The fact that Mr. H has so many possibilities for the investment of his capital surely facilitates the decision-making process; even if a mistake is made, the proposal accepted is profitable.

## APPENDIX D
### Values for Table 4-3

| Proposal | Excess present value as % of cost (discounted at 10%) | Discounted rate of return | Using first year performance to compute Q — Rate of income on total investment | Using first year performance to compute Q — Payback reciprocal | Using average annual returns to compute Q — Rate of income on total investment | Using average annual returns to compute Q — Payback reciprocal | Simple payback reciprocal | MAPI rate of return |
|---|---|---|---|---|---|---|---|---|
| K | .887 | .238 | .181 | .248 | .181 | .248 | .226 | .157 |
| L | .853 | .266 | .257 | .324 | .151 | .218 | .302 | .232 |
| I | .450 | .197 | .136 | .236 | .136 | .236 | .226 | .096 |
| J | .353 | .182 | .147 | .247 | .115 | .215 | .214 | .107 |
| C | .299 | .166 | .111 | .211 | .111 | .211 | .179 | .071 |
| D | .133 | .139 | .175 | .275 | .066 | .166 | .242 | .135 |
| A | .131 | .151 | .098 | .298 | .098 | .298 | .234 | .022 |
| G | .102 | .140 | .091 | .291 | .091 | .291 | .226 | .015 |
| F | .086 | .120 | .136 | .203 | .057 | .123 | .181 | .111 |
| H | .041 | .118 | .136 | .336 | .068 | .268 | .272 | .060 |
| B | —.048 | .080 | .106 | .306 | .045 | .245 | .241 | .030 |
| E | —.148 | .074 | .045 | .112 | .045 | .112 | .090 | .021 |

**VALUES FOR TABLE 4-4**

| Proposal | Excess present value as % of cost (discounted at 10%) | Discounted rate of return | Using first year performance to compute Q | | Using average annual returns to compute Q | | Simple payback reciprocal | MAPI rate of return |
|---|---|---|---|---|---|---|---|---|
| | | | Rate of income on total investment | Payback reciprocal | Rate of income on total investment | Payback reciprocal | | |
| CONSTANT ANNUAL RETURNS | | | | | | | | |
| K | .887 | .238 | .181 | .248 | .181 | .248 | .226 | .157 |
| I | .450 | .197 | .136 | .236 | .136 | .236 | .226 | .096 |
| C | .299 | .166 | .111 | .211 | .111 | .211 | .179 | .071 |
| A | .131 | .151 | .098 | .298 | .098 | .298 | .234 | .022 |
| G | .102 | .140 | .091 | .291 | .091 | .291 | .226 | .015 |
| E | —.148 | .074 | .045 | .112 | .045 | .112 | .090 | .021 |
| DECLINING ANNUAL RETURNS | | | | | | | | |
| L | .853 | .266 | .257 | .324 | .151 | .218 | .302 | .232 |
| J | .353 | .182 | .147 | .247 | .115 | .215 | .214 | .107 |
| D | .133 | .139 | .175 | .275 | .066 | .166 | .242 | .135 |
| F | .086 | .120 | .136 | .203 | .057 | .123 | .181 | .111 |
| H | .041 | .118 | .136 | .336 | .068 | .268 | .272 | .060 |
| B | —.048 | .080 | .106 | .306 | .045 | .245 | .241 | .030 |

# INDEX

Maximum returns: versus adequate returns, 29-30, 91

Miller, David W.: on decisions under conditions of uncertainty, 82n

Miller, James H.: survey of rationing methods, 51

Miller, Merton: on cost of capital, 8n

Minimax principle: case illustration, 79-80; in investment decisions, 79-80, 82-85; usefulness in investment decisions, 82

Modigliani, Franco: on cost of capital, 8n

Morris, William T.: on decisions under conditions of uncertainty, 84n

Most probable future. *See* subjective probabilities

National Association of Accountants: survey of capital budgeting practices, 53

Opportunity cost: as measured by the discounting rate of interest, 14-16

Orensteen, Roger: on computational program for ranking investments, 92n

Payback period: a rationale, 85-90; and break-even analysis, 85-89; and length of life of an investment, 67-68; description of, 22-23

Payback reciprocal: comparisons with other formulas, 30-48; description of, 23-24

Pitfalls: in the use of present value and discounted rate of return, 18-19

Planned: search activity classified and discussed, 93-105

Postauditing: neglect of, 121; usefulness, 6, 11

Present value analysis: and length of life of an investment, 128-30;

Present value analysis (*continued*): and the proper discounting procedure, 126-27; assumptions of, 16, 18-19; comparison with other formulas, 44-48; description of, 13-16; inconsistency with discounted rate of return, 16-19

Programed search: classified and discussed, 93-105

Project life: in investment analysis, 8, 128-30

Qualitative ranking: discussed, 28-29

Raiffa, Howard: on decisions under conditions of uncertainty, 78n, 79n, 81n

Ranking formulas: comparisons of, 30-48

Rate of income on average investment: description of, 24-25

Rate of income on investment: comparison with other formulas, 30-48; usefulness, 121

Rate of income on total investment: description of, 25

Rate of interest: borrowing and lending, 8

Roberts, Harry V.: on discounting rate, 14n

Rose, Joseph R.: on cost of capital, 8n

Ryndall Tire Company: case study, 108-14; evaluation, 114-19

Satisfactory profits: in investment decisions, 29-30, 91

Savage, L. J.: on present value analysis, 13n; on subjective probability, 76n

Schlaifer, Robert: on subjective probability, 84n

Search: classifications, 93-95

Sequential decisions: in investment decisions, 90

Shackle, G. L. S.: on uncertainty, 83

147

Siegelman, Louis: on cost of capital, 7n

Simon, Herbert: on maximum and satisfactory returns, 29; on search, 102, 104-105

Small Business Administration: criteria for small business, 2

Smidt, Seymour: on alternative formulas, 48n; on cost of capital, 7n; on present value analysis, 13n

Smith, Vernon L.: on truck replacement, 123-24

Solomon, Ezra: on cost of capital, 8n; on discounting, 127n; on present value analysis, 13n; on the inconsistency between present value and discounted rate of return, 18

Spencer, Milton: on cost of capital, 7n

Spontaneous: search activity, 93-105

Starr, Martin K.: on decisions under conditions of uncertainty, 82n

Subjective probabilities: case illustration, 76-78; in investment decisions, 76-78, 82-85; usefulness in investment decisions, 82-84

Technological change: effect on discounted rate of return, 75-76

Terborgh, George: on analysis of investment decisions, 2n; on ranking investments, 12n; on

Terborgh, George (*continued*): inconsistency between present value and discounted rate of return, 17-18

Time pressure hypothesis: in investment decisions, 104

Truck leasing company: case illustration, 123, 124

Truck replacement: and uncertainty, 123-24

Trucking firm: case illustration, 89-90

Typewriter company: case illustration, 89

Uncertainty: and break-even analysis, 86-90; effect on investment decisions, 121-22; in investment decisions, 57-92

Usefulness: of various methods of choice under conditions of uncertainty, 76-85

Vending machine company: case study, 141-42; in search for investments, 105

Wearing apparel cases: description, 132-34; involving search activity, 96-97, 105

Wholesale liquor dealer: and search activity, 99-100, 105, 106; case study, 136-40

Willett, Howard: on truck replacement, 124

Working capital: requirements, 10

www.ingramcontent.com/pod-product-compliance
Lightning Source LLC
Chambersburg PA
CBHW022057210326
41519CB00054B/589